ANOTHER AUSTRALIAN EAGLE

The story of an Australian farm boy who became a WW1 Aeroplane Pilot

JOHN P F LYNCH

Published by John P F Lynch

Copyright © John P F Lynch 2023

Lynch, John
Another Australian Eagle

ISBN 978-0-6489446-3-8 (pbk)
ISBN 978-0-6489446-4-5 (e-book)

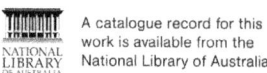
A catalogue record for this
work is available from the
National Library of Australia

The Author of this book accepts all responsibility
for the contents and absolves any other person or
persons involved in its production from any
responsibility or liability where the contents are concerned.

All rights reserved. No part of this publication
may be reproduced, stored in a retrieval system,
or transmitted, in any form, by any means,
electronic, mechanical, photocopying, recording
or otherwise, without prior permission from the author.

Typeset in Bookman Old Style 12 pt

Produced by **TB Books Self-publishing Services**
P.O. Box 8138
Seymour South Victoria 3660
Email: tbbooks@collings.id.au

Cover Design by TB Books Self-publishing Services
Front Cover photo First Australian Airplane made by John Duigan
Back Cover photo by Samrat Maharjan

CONTENTS

FOREWORD v
INTRODUCTION vii

CHAPTER ONE
 The Early Years 9
CHAPTER TWO
 Career Move 33
CHAPTER THREE
 The Light Horse 59
CHAPTER FOUR
 England.. 82
CHAPTER FIVE
 Gallipoli and France 120
CHAPTER SIX
 The Desert.. 145
CHAPTER SEVEN
 Home Again 164
CHAPTER EIGHT
 The Decision... 197
CHAPTER NINE
 A Successful Career...................................... 211
EPILOGUE 236

NOTES 238
AUTHOR 241
OTHER BOOKS By John P. F. Lynch 243

FOREWORD

Another Australia Eagle is the latest in a suite of novels by John Lynch. Set against the backdrop of Australia's early colonial period, it chronicles the life of Jimmy. From his humble beginnings as a mechanic's assistant to becoming an aircraft maintenance engineer and pilot, it explores the relationships and close bonds he forms along the way.

Lynch's attention to detail, combines with his vivid storytelling to form an historical narrative that transports the reader back in time, to when the Australian landscape was filled with endless possibilities for those who strived to reach their fullest potential.

However, there is an emotional core to the narrative that asks the reader to think about the dark side of the history behind the conflict of WW1. Here the characters highlight the impacts of war on the human spirit, during a time when our country was still in the process of forming a national identity.

Lynch's novel is endlessly entertaining, whilst also providing a terrific insight into how previous generations lived, worked and thought about life and country. It is a testament to the power of hope in the face of adversity.

The Hon. Ros Spence MP
State Member for Kalkallo

INTRODUCTION

The first day of February 1901 heralded a new dawn fo the continent named Australia. It soon brought a new vision of progress in governance, industrialisation, agriculture and, in particular, transport.

Motorised vehicles and equipment replaced horses, and steam or combustion engines replaced sail, while quietly in the background, experiments were progressing with 'heavier than air' flying machines.

Many Australians were associated with the land and looked foreward to a prosperous future from their endeavours. However, some were more lateral in their thinking and looked at other enterprises.

Jimmy, the main character in this story, is fascinated by airplanes and the wedge tailed eagle's flight. He follows his aviation dream and succeeds in becoming an engineer and a pilot. He joins the Royal Air Force and eventually is transferrerd to the Australian Light Horse. He serves in both Europe and the Sinai Desert.

Mary becomes a theatre nurse, enlists in the Australian Nursing Corps and is posted overseas to areas of WW1 conflict. She serves on a hospital ship at Gallipoli and in Europe at a casualty post during the carnage year of 1916.

Terry, like many youngsters of this era, joins the Australian military seeking adventure. He serves in both the Western Europe and the Sinai desert battles.

This story relates to historical events that are interwoven with fiction. It gives an insight into the effect WW1 had on the lives of the three country school friends who selected different wartime careers and how they survived those WW1 traumas.

John P. F. Lynch O.A.M.

CHAPTER ONE

The Early Years

The teenage boy lay on the paddock grass, gazing skywards at the two large dark brown birds circling overhead. They swooped down, then soared upwards into the clear blue sky, repeating their aerial acts over and over, gliding on the rising warm air from the heated ground. The birds kept the boy's attention for over five minutes until, suddenly, the pair flew away towards a distant rocky outcrop, a few miles away.

The birds are unique to Australia – the wedge-tailed Eagles. They are an impressive bird with deep, glossy brownish/red feathers and distinctive wedge-shaped tail feathers. The body feathers continue down over their legs. The birds stand proud and erect with their strong head and curved beak. Fully grown, they have a wingspan of around six feet. With these wide long wings, they are capable of floating on air currents for hour-long periods while hunting for food.

These eagles are carnivorous, feeding on rabbits, field mice and other small wild animals and unfortunately, they are of concern to sheep farmers. During lambing time, they will sometimes attack and kill newborn lambs and are often shot because of their folly. The birds are powerful enough to fly for miles while carrying their prey.

An impatient blue heeler cattle dog nuzzled the boy to get up off the grass and head home. Like all active dogs, Bluey was restless. James Symons or Jimmy as he was commonly called, patted Bluey, then walked to his horse grazing nearby.

Jimmy had been fascinated with flying ever since he had read an article on box kites in a magazine he found discarded on a seat in a local rain shelter.

He now collected every story or article relating to flying. He had acquired more knowledge on flight or flying than the average enthusiast.

His most treasured articles were copies of the designs of the American Wright Flyer and some English and French aircraft. He also collected the English Flight magazine.

Jimmy was born in 1894 and lived on a one thousand acre-farm at Wylonga on the Murray River with his mother, Mary, father, Thomas and brother, John.

Thomas Symons and his brother, Michael, had inherited the family farm from their father, who had separated the farm into two five-hundred-acre lots. Michael had left his five-hundred acre lot with the homestead on it for Thomas to manage on his behalf.

Each year Thomas deposited a share of the profits made from the farm into a bank account for Michael, after capital improvements had been deducted. Michael was happy with this arrangement as he had decided his career was to be at sea.

Thomas grazed a mix of Murray Grey cattle and merino sheep on both farm lots. A small vegetable patch, an orchard, a fowl run, and a few milkers had made the family self-sufficient.

The Symons were not wealthy but were comfortable and wanted for nothing. The boys were educated locally and had completed their primary school certificate for grade eight. Jimmy had been Dux of the school in his final year. He had not decided on a career yet, but he dreamed of going to England and joining an aviation firm as a mechanic.

During his last two years of school, on Saturdays, Jimmy would saddle his horse and ride into town to the local garage. He worked there as helper in everything. It served two purposes – pocket money and gaining mechanical experience and technical knowledge.

The garage serviced and repaired all types of mechanical vehicles and machinery devices – steam engines, petrol engines and even push bikes. Jimmy soon grasped the basics of mechanical engineering, including the theory of the combustion engine and steam power. He was mainly involved in dismantling and rebuilding engines, which he enjoyed. He learnt quickly and this was recognised and appreciated by his employer.

The owner was a master mechanic from Melbourne and had immediately recognised Jimmy's aptitude and potential talents. He encouraged him to ask questions at any time to help increase his mechanical knowledge.

Jimmy left school at sixteen years of age and started working full time as an apprentice mechanic, but he had not lost his desire to be involved in aviation. It was constantly in the back of his mind.

He believed the knowledge and practical experience he had gained by working in the garage for four years would be a bonus when seeking employment with an aircraft manufacturing company in England.

The owner made sure that Jimmy kept his daily task log updated, recording all of the various jobs, big or small, that he performed on different types of engines and vehicles he worked on. His father knew of his dream and encouraged him to save his wages for his 'wishful' adventure to England.

During these years, Jimmy kept in contact with his school friends to enjoy some leisure time with them. They would meet on Sunday afternoons at the local park where the local volunteer band played popular tunes to entertain picnicking families and friends. All the locals and sundry enjoyed the pleasant atmosphere. There were varying numbers of his friends who gathered each Sunday, between eight to ten boys and girls. The ones from farms came on their ponies and some of the townies rode bicycles.

Four of them became close friends. Each of them lived on a farm and typically they worked on their parents' farms, particularly during shearing and harvesting times. They could all ride, shoot, fish and had learned to swim in their dams.

Jimmy's farm had a large natural dam in the middle of their property and his father had fenced the larger paddocks in such a way that it provided water to each paddock while keeping the livestock separated as required for breeding purposes or laying fallow.

Jimmy had secret dreams that, one day, one of the paddocks could be used as a landing field for an aeroplane. Unfortunately, neither of his friends were interested in aviation. He had raised the subject once or twice with them, but when he received no questions or comments from anyone, he didn't speak of aeroplanes again.

Eventually he decided to make a kite and launch it in the small paddock. It was alongside a road that divided his farm and one of his friend's farms – Jane Hay. Jane and he were very good friends and often sat together at their weekend gatherings.

Apart from being a tall, very pretty girl with striking titan hair and hazel eyes, she was a very confident, intelligent young woman with an outgoing personality and she was a proficient horsewoman.

Jimmy's other two close friends were Andrew Button, whose father had a sawmill on a small farm, and Ida Whitty. Her parents were graziers. Each were typical Australian teenagers – tall, tanned, content with their lot, and with a love for the country life.

Jimmy's ideal paddock was an elongated rectangle, of some forty acres, fortunately running west to east as the wind direction was predominately from the west – good for flying. The only trees were alongside the fences. Jimmy considered it to be ideal to fly his model aeroplanes and kites. The first kite he made was a copy of an Asian diamond shaped design. It was not an immediate success. It flew with a mind of its own. It spun, twisted and dived headlong into the ground. It performed every manoeuvre possible before it became completely out of control and crashed. After experimenting for several weeks with different length tails, he eventually managed to design a controllable kite.

He normally flew his trial flights on a Sunday afternoon. Sometimes he had an audience parked on the roadside enjoying the sight of the colourful kites, ducking and diving as Jimmy controlled their movements with the long cord attached. By pulling or releasing the tension on the cord he could cause the kite to climb or dive.

The kite design was easy to copy but Jimmy was more interested in a man-carrying flying machine. He was unsure as to what it was that he had learnt regarding the theory of flight. He made several kites of slightly different sizes and shapes and eventually found one particular design was the best. But still his main interest was wanting to be involved in learning how a flying machine capable of carrying a man was designed and manufactured.

His latest design was destined to be his last kite flight. It was a hot gusty day. The strong wind shifted from the west to the northwest and Jimmy was holding the cord in his right hand only. As he reached to pull his hat down tighter on his head with his left hand. A violent gust of wind blew the kite up and across the road, wrenching the cord from his right hand. The kite flew upwards towards a stand of trees alongside Jane's farm dam.

When the gust abated, the kite headed in the direction of the trees and then settled in the upper branches. He stood in the paddock for a while watching to see if the wind would eventually dislodge it. After several minutes he walked down and crossed the road and climbed the fence onto Jane's land, keeping his eye on the kite, watching for any movement.

As he approached the dam, he began looking at the ground to see if he could find the end of the cord. Suddenly, as he reached the dam, he heard girls' voices. He looked up to see two naked girls not ten feet from him, looking up at the kite. When they saw him, they screamed and jumped back into the dam, with the water up to their necks. He immediately realised it was Jane and her sister, Anne. After recovering her surprise, Jane was the first to speak.

She said, 'You startled us; we didn't hear you coming. I guess you're looking for your kite, and you found us as well.'

Jimmy was embarrassed and remained silent. They were the first girls he had seen nude. It had been difficult not to look at them. Both were well developed and had firm breasts. He saw that Jane's titan hair was real. His manliness had been challenged by the sight of their naked bodies. Fortunately, he had his hat to hide it.

Jane continued, 'If you don't mind, please turn around, so we can get dressed.' Even when Jane and her sister were dressed in their cotton dresses, they still showed their femininity. They had no towels and their dresses clung to their wet bodies. The three of them sat together.

Jimmy finally found his voice and laughingly said, 'I'm not sure whether to apologise or say sorry. Because maybe I'm not. You two are beautiful girls.'

Jane laughed. 'Are you going to retrieve your kite today?'

Jimmy's manliness was still of concern. He didn't want to stand up just yet. He replied, 'No. I'll come back tomorrow when the wind has dropped. I'm happy just to sit here and talk.'

After half an hour, he felt comfortable. He stood up and placed his hat on his head, ready to return home. The girls walked with him to the fence and waved goodbye, smiling and laughing.

The next day, he went to retrieve the kite from the tree. It looked almost intact from the ground. He soon found the cord and walked around the trees looking for the best direction from which to pull the kite free.

The wind had shifted to the west and had moderated. He tried twice to free the kite without success. He decided to try once more as Jane rode up on her horse.

After greeting each other, she said, 'I can see it's well and truly stuck. Can I help?'

Jimmy answered, 'Yes, I think you can. You're taller than me on your horse. Can you give it a tug?'

Jane leant forward and took the cord from him and held it as high as she could. She urged her horse forward and after a few seconds hesitation, the kite sprang free and fell to the ground. She clapped in delight. 'We make a good team.'

In the years to come Jimmy would remember those words.

'I can't stay. I'm off to round up some cattle. Bye for now.' Jan rode off with her cattle dog yelping and running alongside her.

The kite had suffered only minor damage – two small tears. These would be easily repaired with linen patches painted over with dope. It had served its purpose, so he decided to stow it in the barn loft. He had already realised the kite was not the answer to a manned flight kit. Wings were the answer, as indicated in his magazines.

As Jimmy walked home, he mused over an incident that had occurred last summer that had bonded Jane and him forever. Seeing her had bought back the memory.

Each year the Town Council organised a regatta on the local lake. It was called a lake but really it was more of a small brick weir. The lake was fed by a creek during heavy rains in the district. The excess water in the lake overflowed the wall and formed a creek lower down.

A few years previous, a concrete wall had been erected on top of the weir to increase the depth of the weir and enlarge the lake surface. The wall was one hundred feet long and fifteen feet deep. The downstream side had five triangular braces set at ninety degrees to the wall. The wall also controlled the water flow downstream to avert flooding. The design allowed for extra concrete blocks to be added in case an increase in the weir wall height was required in the future.

A specially designed crane had been built to position the blocks on the wall and it had been left permanently installed at the weir. The council had no use for it in any other capacity. Surplus blocks had been left there, stacked alongside the crane.

A week before Regatta Day started, dark clouds gathered, dumping heavy rain for three days in the surrounding hills. The lake water volume slowly increased and was expected to rise higher when the upstream waters flowed down into the lake. It was of little concern to the council engineer as he daily monitored the rate of increase in the water height.

The lake was pear shaped with the weir wall situated at the narrow section of the pear shape. The water in the wide, broader section was flowing slowly. To ensure boaters remained in this wider section, two safety lines were attached to several empty air sealed red drums. These lines were tied across the widest section of the lake, clearly visible to all and sundry.

The rain clouds moved on and the spectators enjoyed a clear blue sky, warm glorious sunshine, no wind making the lake water calm. A good day was expected to be enjoyed by all. The first event of the day was a circuit around the lake by the locals in their home designed and decorated boats.

They ranged from homemade native war canoes, pirate ships to bathtubs. Some vessels couldn't complete the circuit and needed to be assisted to shore. Andrew's father had made a four oared dinghy. Andrew and Jimmy rowed Jane and Ida around the course. The girls laid back wearing wide brimmed hats and held large parasols, while waving to the cheering happy crowd. It took the boys a while to co-ordinate their rowing, but they took it slowly and eventually headed smoothly in their desired direction.

The next event was the water fight between the various boats. The four friends weren't interested in this and decided to have their picnic lunch. They pulled the boat from the water and, with help from some nearby spectators, loaded it onto one of Andrew's father's wagons.

They found a flat area alongside the weir wall and sat down on the grass under a flowering gumtree, as the girls served the sandwiches and cakes.

Jimmy spotted Jane's brother, Terry, sitting in a canoe on the wrong side of the safety lines. He was next to the shore, talking with some adults, oblivious to the potential danger.

Andrew suddenly stood up, pointed excitedly. 'Look at the water and the boats. The upstream water is here early. They said it was a day away and we would have no concerns today as the safety lines are in place and all the boat owners had been advised to stay at the top of the weir.' Jimmy stood up and looked to where he saw Terry and his canoe. Neither Terry nor the people he was talking with had seen the rushing waters approaching.

Jimmy began running towards Terry. He yelled and waved his arms. Terry and the others heard him, but by the time they realised what he was yelling, the rushing waters washed the canoe from the shore towards the middle of the narrow section of the lake in a matter of seconds. Terry stayed in the canoe not knowing what to do. Jimmy dived in and swam towards him.

He told Terry to jump from the canoe. It was light, buoyant and was floating fast in the flowing water. Jimmy believed they had a chance if they swam towards the shore. However, the volume of water was too strong and the two of them were swept with the flow.

When Terry jumped into the water, Jimmy managed to hold onto the boy and readied himself to be carried over the weir wall. As they reached the wall, they pressed their legs to the wall to delay the inevitable. Then they vanished over the weir into the swirling waters.

The crowd on the lake banks watched the attempted rescue and gasped in horror when the two of them vanished in the rushing water. Many ran to the other side of the weir wall waiting for them to surface. Some men had stripped ready to dive in and rescue them. After several minutes, concern changed to alarm at the possibility they had drowned, and they would now be looking for their bodies.

A shire engineer stepped forward and asked for volunteers to help move the standby blocks onto the weir wall to try to slow the water volume flowing downstream. The original crane was still in position. Although it had not been used for several years it only required minor maintenance to get it working again.

A mechanic brought grease guns and oil cans from his cart and the crane was soon working. The first block was lifted and slowly positioned. The rushing water was not strong enough to stop the block being placed on top of the wall. The next block required some patience. It was only after several attempts that they managed to get it in place.

The flow of the water downstream had not appeared to have changed. The third block took nearly ten minutes to position. The fourth block placement was proving to be almost impossible.

Suddenly a young boy yelled, 'Look! It's them,' pointing to a corner of the dam wall under where the first block had been positioned.

The engineer took a quick look and confirmed that Jimmy and Terry were huddled together on a concrete ledge about two feet wide.

They were very still and didn't answer calls for them to speak.

The engineer continued showing his leadership qualities. He asked loudly, 'Does anyone have two wide leather or canvas straps?'

A farmer stepped forward. 'I have some draught horse breast straps.'

The engineer answered, 'Get them quickly. I need two strong men to volunteer to be lowered down and lift the boys up.'

Several men stepped forward, but the engineer selected the blacksmith and his adult son. He knew they were strong and would be able to lift the boys safely. The two straps were looped onto the crane hook. The blacksmith and his son sat in one each. It had been decided that both boys would be rescued at the same time. They were concerned about leaving one boy by himself, fearing he might fall into the flowing water.

The blacksmith would look after Jimmy and his son would lift Terry. In the meantime, a doctor and an ambulance had arrived, unsure what to expect.

The rescuers were lowered to be level with the ledge. The boys were still not responding to their questions. They separated the boys who were huddled together. The rescuers hooked one arm under their neck and their other arm bent through their crutch. When they were ready, they gave a thumbs up, the crane lifted them up and then swung them around to dry land.

The doctor took over. The boys' wet clothes were cut from them, and they were then wrapped in thick blankets. They were placed in the ambulance and immediately driven to hospital.

The doctor said little, but he felt a slight pulse in each of the boys. The hospital had beds ready with warmed blankets. The doctor was now able to concentrate on the boys' pulses, body temperatures and alertness. He was very concerned about possible post shock as well as the effects of hypothermia.

When Jimmy dived into the water, it was only then Jane realised he was swimming towards her brother. She could not believe what she was seeing. In a matter of minutes her brother and Jimmy disappeared over the wall in a rush of water. She sat down on the grass in shock. Andrew and Ida had run to the shoreline, watching and hoping.

The next thing Jane noticed was Bill, her father, standing next to her, looking grim. 'Your mother has been taken home and given something to calm her. It's been nearly twenty minutes. I'm hoping for the best but fear the worse. Do you want to go home or stay with me?'

Jane nodded. 'Yes, we stay.' She put her arm in her father's arm and they walked to the dam wall.

Andrew and Ida joined them as they found a spot to sit and watch the concrete blocks being positioned. The sun was now very low. It was nearly two hours since the boys had been swept over the dam wall. The mood was sombre; many had stayed. Out of sympathy, curiosity, or gratitude that they were not in the same situation – who could say?

A loud shout made them stand and move forward to listen to what was being said. They had found the boys. Jane and her father pushed through the crowd and were shocked to see the two boys huddled together in the corner of the dam wall. Neither boy was moving nor answering questions from the engineer.

Jane and her father feared it was the worst result. When the boys were lifted to the shore nobody had a chance to get close to see them. The doctor waited for no one and immediately had them on their way to hospital in the ambulance.

Jane and her father drove to the hospital and sat in the waiting room. Jimmy's parents arrived, bewildered. They had not been at the regatta and had only found out about the drama when a passing friend saw them ploughing in a paddock. He realised that they would have no knowledge of the incident.

It was an hour later when the doctor entered the waiting room and sat down. 'The boys are resting. They both have a very weak pulse, but their temperatures are stable. We are going to monitor them overnight and we will see what tomorrow brings. They have been sedated and a good night's sleep should help them to recover. Drop by here, noon tomorrow. I'll know more by then.' He nodded and left the room.

The two families had known each other for over twenty years. They had never been as close as they were that night.

After a restless night's sleep, both families arrived at the hospital at noon, hopeful for good news. The doctor walked in, smiling. 'It's good news. They are both awake and lucid. I've asked them a few questions – some easy and some difficult. They answered them all to my satisfaction. Their pulses, blood pressures and temperatures are normal. But I am concerned about post traumatic shock. You will need to monitor their behaviour, speech, possible nightmares and extreme restlessness.' He looked around at the families to see if what he was saying was making sense to them.

'They have several cuts and bruises, but these injuries are of no concern. If they continue to improve as they are now, the boys can go home in two days. You can see them now but try to be positive. No tears, if possible! They are in separate rooms now with an assigned nurse. Please come this way.'

Jimmy was sitting up in bed looking out the window. He was rather subdued. He smiled when he saw his parents and his brother, John. His mother rushed to him and hugged him.

His father said. 'You gave us a bit of a fright.'

Jimmy laughed. 'That makes two of us, but I'm good now. How's Terry?'

His father answered, 'He's fine. You both should be coming home in two days.'

Jimmy's mother sat quietly, close to tears but controlling her emotions. They didn't stay too long. After the small talk ended, his parents went home, very much relieved.

The nurse had just finished bandaging his knee and Terry was dozing but he was soon wide awake when he heard his father's voice. He knew Terry was at fault for being on the wrong side of the safety line but now was not the time to discuss it.

His father asked, 'What happened to your knee?'

Terry replied, 'When we went over the wall I landed on my knee and elbow. I felt safe with Jimmy, but the water spray was freezing. The noise was very loud.' He paused for a moment; the memories obviously difficult for him. 'We just sat there waiting for someone to rescue us. Jimmy said they would come. When the water flow slowed over us the first time, we were going to jump. After that I don't remember anything until I woke up in hospital.'

His mother was sitting by his side, holding his hand.

Jane was sitting by herself, close to crying. Her father realised this and decided to leave early.

The next day Jane decided to visit Jimmy. She was exactly what he needed to perk him up. With some fruit and chocolates, she walked into his room and bent over him and kissed him.

He asked, 'What was that for?'

'That was for saving my brother.'

He laughed. 'What about one for saving myself?'

She kissed him again, this time longer.

He sat back and looked at her with admiration. He thought, *One day I will marry you.*

Jane asked straight out, 'Do you want to talk about what happened or do you need more time?'

He was surprised at her forwardness, but he guessed it was typical of her.

He nodded. 'Everything happened so quickly. When I saw Terry was at risk, I dived into the lake without thinking. It was when I reached the canoe, I realized the strength of the water flow. I told him to get out of the canoe and when he did, we watched as the canoe continued to the dam wall.

'We managed to slow ourselves a little in the water flow, but we couldn't reach the shore. Terry had one arm around my neck and his other arm under one of my arms with his hands clasped tightly. As we approached the wall, I knew we would be washed over. I told Terry not to let go of me, no matter what happened. I kept my body upright and when we hit the dam wall, we stayed there for a few seconds but gradually the flow picked us up and we were rolled over the wall.'

He paused for second or two and then continued. 'I couldn't breathe and began to panic and then we landed very hard on the concrete ledge. At first, neither of us spoke. I could see daylight up in a corner where the water wasn't flowing. The noise from the flowing water was loud. I asked Terry if he was alright. I had to shake him to get an answer.' He paused again.

'We were both shaken but he was worse than me. He told me his knee hurt. I laughed. We had nearly drowned, and he was complaining about his knee! I looked at it and could see it was badly lacerated.

'Then Terry asked if we would get out. I thought for a while and told him that we would have to wait, that people would see us in the water and would rescue us. We just needed to remain calm. Then we waited and waited, water spraying us. We started to feel the cold penetrating our bodies. We huddled together and I lost track of time and started to lose consciousness for a minute or so. We crammed ourselves into the corner to ensure, if we did pass out, we wouldn't fall towards the tumbling water.' Jimmy stopped suddenly.

Jane sensibly left the room and came back with two cups of tea. They sat quietly sipping at their cups, each with their own thoughts – Jane grateful Jimmy had saved her brother and Jimmy now realizing how close the two of them had been to drowning.

Jane suggested it was time for her to go but Jimmy wanted her to stay and hear the entire story; he wanted to talk about it. She nodded.

Jimmy took a deep breath. 'I had no idea how long we were on the ledge. I remember vaguely noticing that a small section of the water to the side of the dam wall near us was not flowing. Later the section with no water flowing over the wall widened and we could see out.

'I wanted to call out, but I couldn't talk. I doubt if anyone would have heard my voice over the noise of flowing water, anyway. After that, I have no memory until I woke up here in the hospital.'

Jane told him how the rescue had been organised and carried out under the control of the engineer. When she saw him growing tired she stood up. 'I'll come back tomorrow and see you, but I'll go and see Terry now that I know the full story.' She leant over and kissed him goodbye.

Jimmy was lying in bed dozing, when the doctor walked in. 'You and Terry can go home tomorrow. Before you go, I want you to have a shower. I need to see if you are comfortable standing in a spray of cold water. A nurse will be with you to check your reaction. Don't be embarrassed. They are married and have boys of their own.

'Also tomorrow, reporters will be here to interview you and Terry but not before your parents have arrived. The interview is scheduled for noon. You will be asked a lot of questions and have photographs taken. The engineer, the blacksmith and his son and I have already been interviewed as well as some bystanders. If at any time you want the reporters to stop the questioning tell your father. I must rush now. See you in the morning.'

Terry was awake and reading a comic when Jimmy walked into his room and sat on his bed. He smiled at him. 'How are you feeling? We're going home tomorrow.'

'Yes, the doctor told me. My knee still hurts but I feel good now. I want to go home.'

Jimmy put his arm around the young boy and nodded. 'That makes two of us. I don't like hospitals. We'll soon be home.'

The boys' parents arrived at noon and were introduced to several reporters. Two were from major newspapers and one from the local Gazette. They were seated around a large circular table with the reporters facing the two boys.

Their parents and the doctor were also seated at the table. They were photographed several times – by themselves, together, with their parents, then finally with the doctor and some nurses. The interview was successful. Jimmy related the incident from start to finish virtually with the same words he used to describe the event to Jane.

Choosing his words carefully, a reporter asked, 'How frightening was the experience?'

Terry surprisingly answered immediately. 'Not much. Jimmy looked after me.'

Jimmy thought for a few seconds before replying. 'The worse part was being washed over the weir wall. Before then I wasn't too scared. At first being on the ledge was not too scary but when we began getting very cold, I began to panic. But I knew people would be trying to rescue us. When I first saw the water above us beginning to stop, I felt enormous relief. I knew we would be rescued. After that, I don't remember much – It was just a blur.' He then stopped talking and looked down at the table.

His father put his hand up and said, 'I think that's enough. I'd like the interview to finish now.'

The reporters agreed and thanked the boys and their parents for their cooperation. The doctor had arranged light refreshments for the group to complete the press meeting.

The next morning the local newsagent had people waiting for him to open for trading. Most of the local gazettes were sold within the hour. Some families bought two papers. Thomas Symons was one of them. At dawn, he had ridden into town, as he was eager to know what the city reporters had written about his son.

He rode back into town in the afternoon when the major newspapers arrived. The newspaper headlines were in large print – DRAMATIC RESCUE AT COUNTRY WEIR.

The reporter had slightly exaggerated the drama, but he did write a very accurate description of how the events unfolded. There were five photographs – one each of the boys, one each with their parents and one of the doctor with the two blacksmiths and the engineer.

The rescue was the talk of the town for the next few weeks. Wherever Jimmy went people wanted to shake his hand.

Soon the town got back to normal. Except a lifetime bond had formed between Jimmy and Jane.

When Jimmy arrived home from hospital, the latest edition of FLIGHT had arrived. Previous magazines had mainly focused on diagrams and photographs of kite designs. Later issues now featured monoplanes and biplanes. The kite design had been overtaken by new thinking. Jimmy had already realised the kite had no future with its flying limitations.

When he looked at the wedge-tailed eagle in flight, he knew there was much more to know about controlled flight.

With the rapid increase in improved design of aeroplanes since the Wright Flyer aeroplane flew at Kittyhawk in 1906, more knowledge kept coming to the surface. The theory of flight was evolving – where would it end?

The curve of the eagle's wing intrigued Jimmy. He decided to make a curved diamond shaped kite. It was four feet wide and six feet long, he curved it slightly along the kite's four feet width. He tied a ten-foot long tail of strips of knotted cloth as an experiment and waited for a steady wind – no gusts!

Jimmy's flight test had limited success at his first attempt. The kite ducked and dived a little. It was not completely out of control, but neither was it controllable.

He altered the length of the tail several times and finally succeeded in having the kite steadily siting into the wind.

He then made a kite twice the size of his first kite. He tied a small house brick in the centre of the kite and tried to fly the kite, but the nose of the kite tilted higher than his previous tests and the kite crashed into the field. He experimented by moving the brick further forward. After six attempts he had success.

From the very first of Jimmy's experiments, he made sure to document his attempts and results as he tried to fly his box kite. He thought these notes might serve him well when he applied for employment in the aviation industry in the future.

The wings of the wedge-tailed eagle intrigued him. Their shape changed as they turned or climbed and the small feathers at the wing tips puzzled him. He couldn't quite see what they did. He realized he had a lot more to learn regarding how a bird, not only flew, but how it climbed, dived and turned in flight by only a small movement of its wings and tail feathers.

Summer arrived with a vengeance. Strong winds came from the north with temperatures in the high nineties. Most farmers had cut their back grass and other undergrowth close to their houses and farm buildings and cleared the roof gutters of leaves.

The Symons had empty forty-gallon drums dotted around the buildings area. They had their top chiselled out and then filled with water. Two drums were tied onto a cart and filled with water as a mobile unit. They made up old broom stick handles with small strips of canvas attached. If a fire got close to a building, these canvas sticks would be soaked in the water tubs and the wet canvas sticks would be used to beat the fire out and any embers found alight. It was a simple device, but it worked well as a follow up tool after the fire had passed.

Thomas Symons was watching the smoke billowing on the distant horizon. Even though the wind was moving the smoke away from his property and Bill Hay's, it was still of concern.

He spoke with Jimmy and John. 'There's a bushfire to the northwest and we need to keep an eye on it.

'For the next three or four days, one of us will need to sit here and watch where the smoke heads. Let me know if it changes direction. I'll do the night watch from ten p.m. to eight a.m., John from eight a.m. to four p.m. and Jimmy from four to ten. Don't doze off. All agreed? Good! Let's start.'

He continued, 'Firstly, to be safe, we will move the sheep into the north paddock along the road. It's long and narrow and will make a good fire break. That paddock has been idle for three months and is well grassed and It's now turning brown. Four hundred sheep will soon deplete the grass. Saddle your horses and get your dogs.'

The droving took the rest of the day to complete. Thomas was right. The sheep enjoyed their new paddock and soon reduced the grass, as a possible fire hazard, in a matter of days.

Meanwhile, the fire moved further south and caused damage to some farm shedding and some farmers had livestock destroyed. Fortunately, no homesteads were lost. Jimmy and his father helped other farmers fight the fire. It was typical of the farming community to assist others in time of need.

The fire continued to come from the north. When the fire was about a mile from the road, they moved the sheep down to the long paddock. The large number of sheep had done their job; there was only stubble remaining. Thomas was satisfied. The road was a natural firebreak and if the fire did jump the road, there was virtually no grass to burn. If the stubble were to catch fire, the canvas poles should be able to beat it out and cause the embers to die. It had worked before, and he believed it would work again. Thomas, Bill Hays and some friends watched from the veranda.

When the fire reached the road, it began to burn itself out. Only a few flames managed to jump the road. The men watched and waited to see how far up the paddock the fires would spread. They were small fires and only travelled a hundred feet or so. The paddock was three hundred feet deep.

Smoke was a problem, both from the smouldering stubble and from the fires on the other side of the road. It reached the homestead and made it difficult to see more than twenty feet in front of them. The men decided to attack the burning stubble from the side of the wind.

The water cart was towed by a very reluctant horse. At one stage he was blindfolded to help settle him down. The men made good progress and, as it was getting dark, they decided to stop and just monitor it during the night.

During the afternoon, Thomas went looking for John and became concerned after half an hour. Suddenly John appeared out of the smoke, soaking wet. When asked, 'What have you been up to?' he embarrassedly replied, 'I walked around the corner of the big barn into a dense wall of smoke and in panic, I jumped into a water drum. I thought there was a fire near me.' The men laughed, but all agreed it a sensible thing to do. Better to be safe than sorry. That night was a very stressful one. When the sun set, red glows were everywhere.

The fire over the road had almost burnt out but embers were still alight. The remaining sections of the bushfire had moved to the east by a slight westerly breeze. The fire eventually burnt itself out by not moving. An hour before sunrise, the Symons men were out beating any smouldering stubble. Fire sparks would fly up and quickly burn out. By dawn the paddocks had very few smoking patches. Thomas was an experienced bushman and this bushfire allowed him to show his skills.

Whilst the men were happy. Mary was not, she felt that all the house curtains needed to be washed to remove the smoke smell. Thomas convinced her to open all the windows and doors for a few days and the smell would be gone. Thomas was correct.

The Australian farmers were reared knowing to expect the elements to be difficult. Bushfires, droughts and floods would test them every few years. But they would battle on in the true spirit of their pioneer parents. The Symons and the Hay's families were perfect examples.

CHAPTER TWO

Career Move

At breakfast, they heard a cart horse trotting up their laneway to the front door. It was the local delivery service. Thomas walked down to meet it.

The driver greeted him. 'Good morning, Thomas. I've a letter for you. It arrived yesterday, addressed to: Thomas Symons Esq. I hope it's good news. 'Bye.' He cracked his whip and, with a wave, trotted his horse back down the laneway.

The family rarely received letters. They sat around as Thomas opened the envelope. He commenced reading.

My dear Thomas,

I'm sorry I haven't been in contact with you over the past few years, but as you know, I'm not a great one for writing. I have a small two-room place in Plymouth but I'm rarely there. My only address is the shipping company head office I am with, and I have been with this company for several years now.

I will be in Melbourne at the end of this month as our ship needs some repairs. We had heavy seas in the Australian Bight and damaged a bulkhead.

I still remember the farm as it was from my last visit several years ago. Has it changed much? I can't imagine you not improving it. It's a beautiful farming district.

No doubt the children are now grown up. Give Mary a kiss for me. I plan to arrive at Wylonga, on the 26th. Look forward to seeing you all again.'

Regards to all.
Michael Symons – Chief Engineer
C/O SS Nile
Red Line Shipping Company
Plymouth Dock UK

Thomas sat back and smiled. 'Well! What do you know? Michael's alive and kicking. After so long, it will be good to see him again. We need to get his room ready and freshened up. It hasn't been slept in since he was last here, years ago.' He looked out of the window and recalled the last time he had seen his younger brother.

Thomas rolled the years back. Michael had been born in 1870, four years after Thomas. He became an apprentice to a boilermaker when he was sixteen and went to sea four years later. At the age of twenty-four, he was classed as a third engineer on a small steamship and sailed around Europe for two years. Five years later he joined the International Red Line Shipping Company to crew the SS Nile as their second engineer. He was now the ship's chief engineer. He had not married or formed any long term relationship over these years, although he did have several female friends in Plymouth. Even with their age difference, they had been close as youngsters but when Michael went to sea, ironically, they rarely saw each other again or corresponded. There was no specific reason. It just happened.

In their youth, they went fishing and riding together, as typical Australians lads do. Going to school, they sometimes rode on the same horse. But when Michael fell off and broke his arm, their father stopped them and bought Michael a pony – no more doubling!

As in most schools, fights occur. Michael had fair curly hair and was often teased by his classmates and called 'Goldie Locks.' He resented the name and would take the caller to task – hence a few punches were thrown but with little damage occurring. Thomas never interferred but he did keep an eye on Michael's confrontations.

It was a coincidence that Jimmy was interested in following a mechanical career, like his Uncle Michael's. Although one was a ship's chief engineer and the other one was wanting to start a career as an aircraft maintenance engineer, they had a common mindset.

Jimmy saw the local delivery wagon coming up the driveway, with a passenger sitting alongside the driver. He waved to Jimmy, shouting, 'Hello, young fellow. I guess you're Jimmy.' The wagon stopped and the passenger alighted and walked to him offering to shake his hand. 'I'm Michael, your uncle.'

Jimmy shook his hand. 'I thought it might be you. The family is inside. We were discussing when you might arrive at breakfast this morning.'

They strolled up the path to the homestead.

Jimmy looked at his uncle and commented. 'You have a great beard. It makes you look important.'

Michael laughed. 'Thanks for the compliment, but at sea we have no need to shave. Although, I like to keep mine trimmed.'

Jimmy walked into the kitchen where his family were still having breakfast. 'Look who's arrived – Uncle Michael!'

Thomas, Mary and John stood up.

Thomas said, 'Welcome, baby brother!' They hugged each other in delight at their reunion after so many years separated. Michael then kissed Mary and shook John's hand.

They sat down for breakfast and Thomas asked, 'Well, where do you start with your stories of what you have been up to in the past years?' All eyes turned towards Michael, waiting eagerly for his response.

Michael looked at them and surprised them by saying, 'Well to start, most of my spare time was thinking of being here, and here I am.' He stood up and looked out of the window.

'Yes, I have travelled extensively. It is a good life but at times I feel lonely. The ship is my home and security, although I do own a small apartment in Plymouth for me to stay when the ship is in for maintenance.' He turned and sat down. 'My social life is limited but being a ship's officer has its advantages. I am often invited to formal evenings and functions in foreign ports. Australians are popular in most countries' consuls and embassies.

'I have kept diaries of my sea life from the day I first sailed. I've nearly completed seven annual diaries. In my dotage years I'll read them.

'The first two years, I sailed mainly around the British Isles and the European Channel ports from

Russia to Portugal. Every port has history, and I took every opportunity to visit the famous sites. I've actually become a tourist promotions writer for a London travel company because of my travels to distant lands.' He laughed. 'I really enjoy my journeys. Most of the time the weather is tolerable, even sunny and calm. But the North Sea can be very rough at times.'

He nodded to no one in particular. 'Yes, I have plenty of stories. Once we had engine trouble in the North Sea.'

He thoughtfully proceeded. 'We were tossed around by very large waves for several hours until we managed to repair the problem. Once we ended up with several crew incapacitated with broken bones and severe bruising. The sea can be obliging but also demanding and even frightening.'

Uncle Michael stopped talking and began to eat his breakfast.

Jimmy asked, 'What type of training did you have and what type of engines do you work on?'

Michael finished his cup of tea before answering. 'I started as boiler mechanic and over the years learnt from my senior engineers, practical training and studying the engine manufacturers' manuals. Eventually I passed my Maritime Board Examination. One thing about being at sea – you have plenty of time to study.'

Jimmy's dad interrupted, 'Let your uncle finish his breakfast. There's plenty of time for talking.'

After breakfast, Thomas hitched up a buggy and took Michael for a ride around the farm and the district. It was a pleasant sunny day with plenty of bird life chirping in the gum trees and flowering scrubs.

The paddocks were dotted with livestock and a few kangaroos lay in the shade of the trees.

Michael commented, 'Nothing seems to have changed except for a few more houses and shops in town and bigger trees in the main street.'

Thomas nodded. 'Yes, it's still a cosy and friendly little town and typical of the Australian bush. I hope it remains so. Incidentally you have a very healthy bank account.'

Michael smiled. 'I'm not interested in retiring yet.'

They arrived back at the farm in time for lunch. Jimmy made sure he sat next to his uncle, intending to ask him more questions.

Thomas realised what Jimmy intended. 'Jimmy, after lunch you can have a one on one with your uncle. No questions during lunch.'

After lunch Jimmy went to his room and retrieved his collection of aviation material and laid it out on the dining room table. Michael saw him entering from his room and after about five minutes he followed him. He had guessed this was to be the time to talk.

Michael sat down. 'Ask away.'

Jimmy didn't need a second invitation. 'I want to work on aeroplanes, and I have been collecting any information I can find in magazines, newspapers and books.'

Michael interrupted. 'First, tell me what you have been doing since you left school.'

Jimmy handed his uncle his daily work logs which he had diligently completed each day since he started working. Michael read each page, sometimes nodding or saying 'um' to himself. Jimmy sat quietly.

After five minutes Michael looked up. 'Good. You have a wealth of practical experience in mechanical engineering, and you have good reports on your performance.'

He then asked, 'Where do you want to go from here? I can see you would have few opportunities in Australia. As you already know there are several European aeroplane manufacturers competing with their new designs and ideas to attract potential operators. Without doubt, it's a new industry, and it's growing quickly.'

He turned his attention to Jimmy's collection of books, papers, pamphlets and magazines. Without commenting, he browsed through them. He finally looked up and said, 'Well, you are obviously very interested in aeroplanes. You have a very impressive collection of aeroplane data!'

Michael continued, 'I don't like to say it, but if you really want a career in the aviation industry, you should consider going to Europe. I presume you have given it some thought?'

Jimmy nodded. 'Yes, I'm saving up, but I don't earn much, and it will take me at least another year to have enough money just for a ship's passenger ticket.'

Michael interrupted. 'Have you discussed this with your father?'

Jimmy replied, 'Well, sort of. I think he considers me too young to travel overseas. He might listen to you. What do you think?'

Michael replied, 'Yes, we three could discuss it.'

Three days later, after lunch, his father called Jimmy into the lounge room where his mother and Uncle Michael were already seated. 'Your uncle has been telling us of your wish to travel to Europe to join the aviation industry. I know you have mentioned it to me twice before and I was non-committal. Your uncle is very impressed with your explanation of why, and with your aeroplane technical knowledge and feels you are sufficiently mature to travel overseas. Obviously, your mother and I are concerned. It's a big decision for you to make. Your uncle has something to say.'

Jimmy looked at him, holding his breath. He knew the family had come to a decision.

Michael nodded. 'By saving towards your passage to travel overseas, you have shown how keen you are to go to Europe. The aeroplane knowledge and mechanical experience you have acquired is a very big plus.' He looked straight at Jimmy.

'As you know I am the ship's chief engineer. I have a vacancy for a 'Grease Monkey.' The name describes the job. His job is to oil and grease all moving parts in the engine room. The pay is low, but you will have good food and a bunk. It will get you to Europe and you will have your savings and money earned on the ship in your pocket. Also, I have a library of engineering manuals you can borrow to read in your leisure hours. You can leave your collection in my cabin, if you wish.'

He paused, allowing his comments to sink in. 'Furthermore, I have a friend who is a draughtsman, who sometimes does part time work for a factory assembling experimental aeroplanes for the Avro Airplane Company. I could write you a letter of introduction to him and maybe he could point you in the right direction for your employment opportunities. Think over what I've said. I'll be leaving next Monday to return to my ship. We sail two days later.'

Jimmy sat quietly, hardly believing what he had just been told. He stood up and shook his uncle's hand. 'Thank you.' And then he hugged his mother and father – thanking them, too.

He walked outside and sat on the veranda. Looking down the paddock, he saw a wedge-tailed eagle soaring up into a low cloud. He took that as a good omen for his future.

The next morning Jimmy felt a sense of peacefulness. He was going to Europe. He went to the barn to find a box for his collection of technical data. Up in the loft were several old military chests that were there when his grandparents purchased the property. The smaller one would suffice for the data and the larger one for his clothes.

Jimmy's mother laid all his clothes out on his bed. She commented, 'I think you and I need to go shopping for some winter clothes. We can go into town tomorrow.' Within two hours of arriving in town his mother had visited every clothing shop in the small town and purchased him a complete set of winter attire.

One shop was owned by a Scot from Glasgow, and he gave good advice. 'In very cold weather, it's not the thickness of a garment that counts, it's the layers of the clothes you wear and always buy wool vests and pullovers. Wear a woollen bonnet or cap and gloves whenever you can, plus have good footwear and keep an oilskin coat handy. Always aim to be warm and dry.

'In England you will be able to buy a double jacket. That is, one jacket fits inside an outer jacket. It's worth having during the snow season.'

Jimmy listened to this advice and would remember it.

On the way home, Jimmy's mother asked him if he had told Jane he was going overseas yet.

He shook his head. He knew he had to tell her. He decided he would ride over the next day and see her. He wondered how she would react, as he realised she was fond of him – maybe more than fond!

He knew he would miss her, but his ambition for a career in aviation must come first. If he didn't try, he would spend the rest of his life regretting it. Where would that leave Jane? Would they both be blameless because of his lost career opportunity?

Jane saw him riding up the lane to the house and gave him a wave. She walked down the steps and took the reins and wrapped them over the hitching rail. She smiled at him. 'To what do I owe the pleasure of this visit?'

Jimmy put his arm around her shoulder. 'I need to tell you something.'

Jane stopped smiling. 'You sound serious!'

He looked at her, suddenly unsure how to tell her. He took a deep breath. 'I'm going to England next week to find a job working on aircraft.'

Jane sat quietly, absorbing what Jimmy had said. After a few moments she looked at him and replied, 'I should have known that one day you would go to England. I'll miss you. I had hoped we would have a future together.' She started to cry.

Jimmy put his arms around her, uncertain what to say. Finally, 'I need to do this, or I'll regret it until my dying day and yes, if I were older, I would ask you to marry me. I have always wanted to be with you. I would come back for you but I don't think I have the right to ask you to wait, when I don't know what the immediate future holds for either of us. I would ask you to wait but it would be unfair.'

Jane composed herself and replied, 'I believe I could wait for you, but we would need to keep in contact and be honest with each other.' She stood up. 'Let's walk.' She held his hand as they headed down the lane, not saying a word.

Jimmy spoke first. 'Will you wait for me?' He turned to her and kissed her gently.

She responded with, 'Yes, I will.'

He said, 'Mum is having a farewell dinner. I'd like you to come.'

The farewell dinner was a mixture of happiness and sadness, happy chatter and farewell speeches. Michael was in his element with his witty speeches and apt comments. The family presented Jimmy with a gold engraved watch and Jane gave him a ring with two entwined sections.

Jane was delighted with the gold locket he gave her.

He made a short speech of thanks to a very quiet audience. Each had their own thoughts regarding Jimmy's future.

That night was to be the last time he would see Jane as a teenager. Michael gave Jimmy a wide leather belt with pockets sewn into it. It was to be worn under his outer clothes to keep money and papers secure. It would prove its value in the years to come.

The chests were loaded onto the coach. The farewells were quick, a few tearful kisses and handshakes and a crack of the whip and Uncle Michael and Jimmy were driven to the railway station. It was a Monday morning with few people around. A few knew he was leaving and gave him a wave. They had the train carriage compartment to themselves.

The journey was pleasant. A sunny day, green paddocks and newly shorn sheep made for a typical Australian rural scene. Michael probably enjoyed it more than Jimmy, after being away from Australia for so long. When the train was running parallel to a road, often school children and other road users would wave. The train gradually began to fill with passengers as it got closer to Melbourne.

Michael was in his engineer officer's uniform and looked a little out of place on a country train. He had a war ribbon on his uniform, that he had been awarded during the Boer War when his ship was seconded by the British army for twelve months to deliver troops and supplies to South Africa.

It was late afternoon when they reached Melbourne. They walked to the baggage car and unloaded their luggage. A coach soon pulled up looking for business. Jimmy was now becoming a bit apprehensive.

Michael sensed the feeling and said, 'When you are asked how you were recruited, tell them I saw you in our city office and after talking with you, I offered you the job of 'grease monkey' as you want to go to England to get a job.' Jimmy nodded.

'Tell them, it's a cheap way to get there to find a job on aeroplanes,' he continued. 'I don't want you calling me uncle. It's best the crew don't know you're my nephew. You are always to call me "sir". You will be answerable to the chief stoker. He's tough but fair. You can learn a lot from him.' Jimmy nodded he understood.

He could smell the sea air. It was different from the country and Melbourne city. It seemed cleaner and fresher but lacked the smell of the country trees. They rounded a street corner and he saw Port Phillip Bay for the first time – a wide sandy beach with the blue water of the bay vanishing into the distance.

His uncle pointed to the pier where three ships were busily loading cargo. He said, 'The red hulled ship is ours – the SS Nile.'

Jimmy was surprised that it was so big. Above the main deck were two levels of quarters and atop the forward upper deck was the bridge. Two tall funnels protruded aft on the forward upper deck.

The coach stopped alongside some loading nets. They put their chests into the nets to save carrying them up the gangway.

The chief stoker had seen the coach trotting down the pier. When it stopped, he walked over to Michael and said, 'Welcome back, sir. I trust you had a good break.' They shook hands.

Michael answered, 'Yes, excellent, but it will be good to get to sea again. I have a new grease monkey I hired for you. Meet Jimmy Symons. Jimmy, this is Chief Stoker Bill Hill; he's your boss. I'll leave you with him.' He turned and headed up the gangway and disappeared inside the ship.

The chief stoker said to Jimmy, 'Follow me. We'll collect your gear later. You need to carry out the administration requirements first. And call me sir. Actually, it might be a good idea to call everyone sir, until you know otherwise. Most crew are ex-navy from various countries, but they still observe rank or an equivalent position. It's a good habit and ensures discipline.'

He knocked on a cabin door labelled "Executive officer". 'Come in,' greeted his knock.

A tall middle-aged man stood up and asked, 'What can I do for you, Chief?'

'A new recruit needs to give you his details.'

He nodded. 'Sit down, young fellow, and tell me about yourself.' After half an hour of talking and answering questions, Jimmy was asked to sign some papers. 'Welcome aboard.' The officer shook his hand and dismissed them. He left with the chief, who had remained during the interview. He now knew of Jimmy's history and his reason to join the ship to travel to England.

The chief took him to his office. 'Well, you're an interesting young fellow and well educated with good engineering knowledge. By the time we reach England you'll probably have my job. Now to business! Firstly, here is a diagram of the ship's company, from captain down. Secondly, here is a diagram of the ship, its decks and the engine room. We don't sail for two days.' He looked directly at Jimmy. 'I want you to study them during this time and remember every detail. Now about your job – it is dirty and boring but important. If you stuff up, I will come down on you like a ton of bricks. Any questions?'

Jimmy answered, 'Not yet.'

'Good. Follow me; I'll show you your quarters.'

He was shown a very large cabin with a single row of bunks on each side. There were two tables in the centre.

Under the bunks were two large drawers for stowage of clothes and personal items. Two sailors were sitting at one of the tables drinking tea.

The chief introduced Jimmy to them as Fred and Danny and then left after saying, 'Be at my office at zero nine hundred hours, the day after tomorrow. In the meantime, familiarise yourself with the ship.'

The two sailors were friendly and asked a few questions, such as where he was from and what was he. Jimmy answered honestly that he was working his passage to England for a job on airplanes. The other two were full time sailors.

Danny explained the daily routine. 'The galley is next door and meals are brought to the cabin table by a steward at zero eight hundred hours, noon and eighteen hundred hours. Tea breaks are flexible depending on your workload. Lights out at twenty-two hundred hours. There are three other cabins like this. One is for watch keepers to have an uninterrupted eight hours' sleep. It's a happy ship and your boss is good. The officers are all respected and very professional. It's one of the best ships I've sailed on.'

Fred commented, 'He's right. Do your job and you'll be fine. Take the bunk at the end.'

Jimmy collected his gear, unpacked it and stowed it in his drawers. He poured himself a cup of tea and began to study the diagrams of the ship and the decks and, in particular, the engine room. After an hour, he decided he had studied enough, and he should write to Jane.

He only wrote a short letter. Mainly he described the ship and the people he had met so far. He told her he loved her and missed her already. The ship had a mailbox, which was cleared each day when in port and sometimes was transferred at sea to another ship heading to the letters' destination.

Two days later as instructed, Jimmy reported to the chief stoker, who smiled, saying, 'Good morning, young fellow. Let's get you to work.' He followed him down to the engine room, which was a hive of activity.

He signalled to a stoker, who came forward. The chief said to Jimmy, 'This is John Brown. He's the shift supervisor and your boss. I'll leave you with him.'

John shook his hand. 'Come with me.' He showed Jimmy a grease gun and oiler and gave Jimmy a chart of the engine room. 'Your job is to grease or oil the items on this chart every day we are at sea. I will check your performance every now and then, and I will not be impressed if you miss any of them. Don't be backward in asking questions. Away you go; start now. I'm very busy at this moment. We'll have a chat later today.'

Jimmy went to the bow and walked around the main deck trying to absorb each and every detail of the ship. As the ship was preparing to sail soon, he could sense the urgency in the crewmen's activities. Cargo and food stocks were being craned into the holds and packed tightly and neatly.

He proceeded to the lower decks and soon got lost. Eventually he found the access to the engine room. As he was studying his chart, a stoker approached him and asked, 'Are you the new grease monkey? I'm Jake, this shift's leading stoker.'

Jimmy nodded. 'Yes, I'm identifying where the greasing and oiling nipples are.'

Jake replied, 'It will take time, but you can't miss any when we're at sea. Let me know if you have any problems. You will join my crew tomorrow. See you then.'

The engine room was noisy and claustrophobic. The walkways were mainly metal grates with some areas having safety handrails for inclement weather. With the heat and smells it was surprisingly very clean. It took him several hours to locate all the grease and oil points. He realised that he would need the chart for quite a while. There were forty points to remember.

At the end of the day a whistle sounded and the crewmen and shoremen finished work for the day. Jimmy headed back to his cabin. Fred and Danny were there chatting in a group. Danny introduced him to them. They were a variety of crewmen – seamen, cooks, stokers, stewards and even a male nurse. He was an ex-Army medic.

As a country boy, Jimmy was a little reserved at first but soon felt comfortable to be with them.

The next morning, Jimmy presented himself to Jake, holding his chart in his hand. Jake said, 'I'll show you how you grease and oil. Then you can take over. Take your time and don't skimp on the grease or oil. Let's go.' After ten or so minutes, Jake asked, 'Did you follow my examples?'

Jimmy said, 'Yes, I can do it. I'll be right.' Jake left and Jimmy was now a real grease monkey.

He took nearly five hours to complete the greasing and oiling. Some areas were difficult to access and some dangerously near moving parts. He could see that the job would be difficult in rough seas. When the whistle sounded, he headed to the showers. His overalls were mainly covered in oil and some grease.

That night he wrote to Jane. It would be the last letter he would post in Melbourne as they were to sail the next day. He explained his job on the ship. He was happy even if it was probably the worse job aboard. He was going to England and being paid. It was not much but it would add to his savings.

Already he felt lonely, but he had several photographs of her and his family. He looked at them often to remember their smiles and voices.

The day of departure was exciting for him. He stood at the bow and watched as the ship was pulled away from the dock by a tugboat. He could feel the engines throbbing below deck and see the smoke emanating from the smokestack. The wind was mild and from the west, creating small two-foot high waves.

The ship slowly increased speed, heading south towards the notorious Port Phillip Bay heads. He went below to the engine room and completed his greasing and oiling tasks quickly and then went up on deck. The wind strength had picked up and the waves were higher with white crests foaming at their tops. The ship was pitching and rolling, but not too uncomfortable for a new crewman like himself.

Jimmy noticed that with the ship's movements, he had to walk differently. He stepped slowly and softly on the deck. It took him a few days to feel comfortable walking on board.

'Good afternoon, Jimmy. How are you settling in?' It was Michael standing alongside him.

'Hello, sir. Yes, I'm happy. I'm being well treated and helped. I feel part of the crew already.'

Michael pointed ahead. 'See the gap between the two headlands? They're called "the heads". We will be going through them on the top of the outgoing tide. We'll be using our own power but helped by the tidal waters pouring out of the bay. You'll see churning waters all around and then feel the ship's speed increase.

'The ship will be out in Bass Strait in about half an hour. I haven't sailed out of the heads for many years, but I can still remember those thrilling scenes. We can watch it together and you can write home about us sharing the moment.'

Jimmy nodded, not taking his eyes from the approaching bay's two headlands over the ship's bow.

Slowly he felt the ship move differently. The ship was now on the outflowing tide. It was turbulent, causing the ship to roll and pitch more. The sea was foaming and swirling. Jimmy could see the seawater pouring out on the seaward side of the headlands into Bass Strait. Soon it was all over. The ship was clear of the heads' high tidal outflow. It then turned west heading towards the Great Australian Bight. This course headed the ship into the "Roaring Forties", the notorious strong and unpredictable winds. The next few weeks taught Jimmy how to be a sailor.

He was seasick a few times but soon learnt to look at the horizon when on deck and not the rolling white capped seas.

He wrote to Jane every fortnight, not that there was much to tell, but write he did, even if he repeated his sentences. He wrote mainly about his duties and the sea scenes.

Sometimes they transferred mail at the port they had just departed, to a passing ship. Hopefully she would receive them within a few weeks.

The trip through the Great Australian Bight was rough. At times the sea spray covered the ship. His job as grease monkey was difficult. He was thrown about several times and often lost his balance. He had bruises on bruises. The medic gave him some salve to ease the pain.

Jake was aware of Jimmy's discomfort but wisely left Jimmy to himself.

Two other crew members suffered broken bones when some cargo pallets broke their restraints, when they were bringing food up for the galley, and another had incurred a badly gashed head when an unrestrained box fell from an overhead bin. The strong winds and rough seas continued for two more days and then the weather changed dramatically – calm seas and warm sunshine.

Some evenings, Jimmy would sit on a forward bollard and enjoy the breeze on his face, ignoring his bruised body.

They were scheduled to transit Colombo in Ceylon, then Aden, Cairo, Naples and then direct to Portsmouth. The ship would bypass Fremantle. They were out into the Indian Ocean, en route to Ceylon when the fateful news of war being declared was announced.

The ship's captain addressed the crew. 'I regret to advise you, I have received a telegram from our head office, stating that England and Germany are at war from this day. I'll stay on this course, unless otherwise instructed. However, with immediate effect, two lookouts will be rostered to watch out for other ships. We will avoid any contact with unidentifiable ships. That is all. I shall keep you updated as necessary.'

The mess deck was a hub of voices. Was the captain worried there could be German naval vessels in the area? Some crew knew there were British warships based in Ceylon. The mood gradually became pensive. Two crewmen were German and were quietly asked to report to the bridge. They were questioned by the executive officer regarding any family members who were in the German Military Forces or members of the Nazi Party.

He received a negative answer. After further discussion they were allowed to continue their ship duties. They had over ten years' exemplary service with the company. This stood them both in good stead. They were ordered not to go near the radio room.

The radio operator was ordered not to leave the radio room without an officer's permission, and the door was to be locked day and night. He now sat with his headset on continuously, listening for other ships' transmissions. He would only answer a head office message, requiring a response.

The next few weeks proved rather boring, after the excitement of war being declared.

Michael walked up to Jimmy one day and asked, 'How are you settling in? Are you studying?'

Jimmy admitted, 'No, I haven't been studying, but I will, I promise you and I am enjoying the job. It's easy. I'd like to be doing something more demanding.'

Michael said, 'I'll mention it to the chief stoker. Bye for now.'

Jimmy was watching some flying fish skipping the wave tops when he spotted two albatross birds gliding above the ship. He was intrigued by their wings, particularly the wing tip feathers. Their wing curvature was not unlike the eagle, but their wings were longer and narrower. He sat there and memorised their shape and wing tip feathers. *[NOTE 1]*.

He suspected that an eagle's wings were made more for speed and diving, whereas the albatross's wings were designed for gliding. He later recorded his thoughts in his aviation logbook.

He began to study again. Michael had loaned him an abbreviated maintenance manual on the ship's engine. After four weeks of concentrated daily studying, he felt he was competent to pass an examination. He was pleased he was working in the engine room every day and had learned to identify the engine parts and the controls. He then began reading through his collection of data and continued to do so until the ship docked in the UK.

Jake approached Jimmy. 'I believe that you would like to be involved in a job more interesting, as well as being a grease monkey.' Jimmy nodded.

Jake replied, 'At times, we're required to change engine components due to failure or time expired. When this work is required, I'll include you in the work team.'

Jimmy replied, 'Thank you. That will be great.'

They enjoyed the Indian Ocean journey. The seas were moderate, the sky had very little cloud and there was plenty of sunshine.

Some sailors, in their leisure time, sat with fishing lines tied around their wrists as they dozed in the sunshine. A tug on the line soon had them fully alert again. One sailor caught a small shark. The cook served it for diner that evening.

Ceylon was a welcome sight after so long at sea and out of sight of land.

Jimmy had seen a few aborigines on the Murray River but was intrigued by the small, very dark Ceylonese people. He soon regained his land legs and was surprised, when he visited a market, to find that they spoke English fluently. They were very polite and friendly. He and Jake hired a local cart to see the sights. The various temples were impressive, as were their worshippers in their different attire.

The beaches were pristine clean golden sands, blue seas and rolling surf. Palm trees dotted the shoreline, amid small cottages. Late afternoon they headed back to the ship and enjoyed a good night's sleep.

They stayed in Colombo for two days, then headed to Aden at the entrance to the Red Sea. The ship's company were still on alert and became nervous as they approached the African mainland. Several ships were seen on the horizon, heading on a similar course, no doubt sailing to the Suez Canal. Radio silence was strictly observed, even when the ships appeared to be genuine transports.

They arrived at Aden harbour and kept a watchful eye on the other mooring ships. A representative of the British Foreign Office came on board and met with the ship's captain and some his officers. He advised them that the other ships were not German but genuine transports. The German Raiders were not expected to be sufficiently foolhardy as to attempt to travel up the Suez Canal!

Aden was a British port with a large British population. The town was hot, dry, sandy and brown. Both the roads and the buildings were the same colour and appeared to be made of the same material.

The houses were mainly two story. The top story had large window sized cut outs. The lower floor hot air would then rise and escape, while fresh cooler air would be sucked into the updraft, and the cycle was repeated.

The crew were invited to several afternoon gatherings, arranged by the local families. One event was a cricket match. Jimmy played, managing to score twenty runs. Most of the crew were pleased to leave Aden.

The town not only looked dirty, but it also felt unclean and unfortunately swimming in the harbour was a no-no, due to sharks.

A day later, they sailed up the Red Sea to Port Suez. The Suez Canal and been built in the mid 1800's. It was in two parts, each a single canal. *[NOTE 2]*

Port Suez to the inland lake at Ismailia was the first part. Their ship would then wait its turn to enter the second canal, which went from the Ismailia lakes to Port Said in Egypt. The Red Sea separated Africa and Saudi Arabia up to Port Suez.

After dinner, Jimmy went up on deck. His timing was perfect to see one of the most impressive sights in the world. Every sailor needed to experience the sun setting over Africa. The extraordinary colours had to be seen to be believed. The Red Sea with the desert and palm trees as a backdrop has the setting sun meeting it. No camera could capture the magnificent multicolours of reds through to yellows of the sunlight, as it slowly vanished beneath the desert horizon.

Jimmy became aware he was not the only person watching the sight. Over twenty other crewmen were on deck viewing the same scene. The Red Sea was an appropriate name.

Port Suez Canal appeared on the bow. A narrow stretch of water disappearing into the distance with a desert either side. The ship's speed was reduced to eight knots. Excess speed would generate bow waves which could damage the canal walls. The trip was boring. Jimmy had expected to see Arabs and camels. There were only a few villages to be seen. Nothing of note.

Until they reached the three connected Bitter Lakes and Ismailia.

Ismailia, a city of interest was on the west side of the northern most lake. The town management controlled the movement of the ships. Several other ships were dotted around the lake. Some were waiting to sail to Port Suez and others waiting to sail to Port Said. They moored, waiting for their turn to enter the canal.

Jake called Jimmy over. 'While we're moored, we're going to change a generator. Come to the engine room at noon.'

Jimmy nodded. 'Yes, for sure.' At last, a different job. He would be one of a team of four.

The generator was due to have its commutator segments skimmed. It was normal wear due to the generator's rotors continual contact with the carbon brushes. The brushes would be changed at the same time. The generator would be moved by an overhead crane. It was too heavy to manhandle.

After disconnecting the electric cables, the team attached the sling to the crane, unbolted the generator and slowly removed it from the gearbox. The overhead crane moved the generator out of the engine room and into a workshop where the generator was lowered onto a cradle attached to the deck, where it was strapped down. A new generator was installed repeating the removal process.

Jake asked Jimmy to remove the brushes' cover and remove them, while the other three crew handled the replacement generator installation. Jimmy was pleased to be given a task. He felt he was being tested and he was! The task was easy, and he soon had the brushes removed and laid out on a bench for Jake's comments. While waiting, he examined the commutator and was surprised at how little wear there was to the copper segments.

Jimmy felt only a little undercutting between the segments was necessary. The chief engineer, his Uncle Michael, agreed. After Jake and Jimmy undercut the mica grooves, they evened the segments. New brushes were fitted and the generator declared ready for service. Jimmy was given a few more tasks after his performance with the generator.

The winching of the anchor was noisy as it was hauled up and stowed in the chain locker. The ship was soon creating a small bow wave as it gathered speed. They now headed into the Port Suez end of the canal at a steady speed of eight knots. Another ship was ahead of them, about a mile distant, and another followed them a mile behind. The scenery was still boring, but it was thrilling sailing up the famous canal to Cairo albeit Egypt. Slowly small settlements appeared in the distance. Palm trees, camels and tents, even some sand-coloured houses. Port Said was a disappointment. It was large and drab. Fortunately, palm trees and other greenery helped make the city more appealing.

Jake and he went ashore for a break from the ship. They visited a bazaar to buy a few souvenirs and then returned onboard. Most of the crew didn't fancy Port Said and were glad they left after a stopover of two days.

When in open waters, their ship joined a fleet of merchant ships and warships. The warships were on the outside of the merchant ships and were darting around like mother hens, keeping every ship informed. Submarines were a major concern in the Mediterranean Sea. Each ship had Admiralty orders in case of an attack.

The SS Nile had two guns mounted, one at the bow and the other on the stern deck. They had been fitted in Colombo. Four Royal Navy gunners had also been transferred to the SS Nile to operate them, if needed. Some crew had been trained to assist.

The remainder of the crew were trained to operate as firemen as directed, if they were hit by shells. Although everyone was on edge for the entire crossing. Nothing happened, not even an alert.

The Rock of Gibraltar loomed out of the mist. An enormous triangular, seven hundred and fifty foot high ridge of limestone, bordering Spain. It was a heavily fortified British Air Force and Naval base at the entrance to the Mediterranean Sea.

Jake pointed out the close African country of Morocco opposite Gibraltar. Spectacular and impressive, the Rock was an important British possession as it controlled entry to the Mediterranean Sea.

The convoy and the SS Nile sailed onto the UK. The skies were clear and when two German aircraft appeared to the west, the gunners assembled their crews. Fortunately, the aircraft turned away.

Michael came to see Jimmy to make sure he had packed the books he had left in his quarters. They would arrive at Portsmouth within two days.

Jimmy had enjoyed the voyage but would be glad it was over. He had learnt new skills and felt he had matured in confidence and attitude. He wondered what was next for him in his search for his career.

Michael appeared at his side and pointed. 'We're here; there's England.'

CHAPTER THREE

The Light Horse

When war was declared, Jane's brother, Terry, was one of the first Victorians to volunteer to join the Australian Light Horse. He was very fortunate. He was in Melbourne when it was announced and was staying near the Victoria Barracks.

From his window, he could see workmen erecting signs, "Recruiting Office", on the roadside. He dressed quickly and ran to the barracks, where a queue of fifty or so men were already assembled.

The sergeant, Ian Norris, carrying out the interview, recognised the name Bill Hay as Terry's father and the town, Mylonga. 'I sheared there in years gone by and served with your father in the Boer War. I can understand why you want to join the Light Horse. I know that all of you lads in the farming district could ride at a very early age.'

After a successful medical examination, Terry was enrolled. Norris advised Terry he would receive a letter in a few days to report to Broadmeadows Army Barracks. As an eighteen-year-old lad, he was most proud, and he hoped his family also would be.

In Melbourne, thousands of able-bodied men volunteered in the first weeks. Many were unlucky as the initial quota was quickly reached. Most would reapply, successfully.

When he was travelling home, Terry thought of his parents' reaction. Should he have discussed it with them? Well, it was too late to worry now.

When he told them, his mother cried a little, but his father shook his hand. 'I'm proud of you. Well done, following in my footsteps.'

The official letter arrived the following week. He was to report to the barracks the following Monday with a minimum of clothes.

He made a few farewell visits around town to school friends and found others were considering joining the Australian Army.

When Jane was told, she suggested to Terry to start writing to Jimmy. 'Who knows, perhaps you'll meet up in the big wide world.'

Terry agreed. That night he wrote to Jimmy telling him of his decision in joining the Australian Army.

The farewell at the station was the same old – tears, kisses, handshakes and hugs.

His father handed him some newspapers to help pass the time. The town of Broadmeadows was about twenty miles north of Melbourne.

Terry was both apprehensive and excited as he waved goodbye from the carriage window. The train trip was boring as usual.

At the railway station, it was shambles. Soldiers yelling and screaming out orders. Terry eventually found himself with a group of totally confused recruits. When the soldier yelled, 'Line up in rows of three and follow me.' They did.

After a trek of three muddy miles, they arrived at a tent city that continued forever. The soldier, a corporal, told them, 'I'm the boss of you motley lot. When I say jump, you will jump! Do you understand? I can't hear you.'

The recruits all started shouting, 'Yes. We hear you, corporal.'

The corporal continued. 'Each tent is numbered. I will call out your name and tent number, you will go to that tent and remain there.' When the corporal finished calling out names, three recruits remained.

Terry was one of them. 'Follow me.' They followed. The corporal stopped to talk to another corporal. 'These three are yours, Bill. They're Light Horse recruits. Bye.'

The new corporal was older and looked wiser. 'Welcome to our disorder. Believe it or not it was worse last week, when it rained non-stop. I'm Corporal William Jones and I will introduce you to the Army. I'll teach you your right foot from your left, how to march, how to shoot, who to salute and the Army Regulations you need to be aware of. I am fair but don't cross me. You have been warned. Now that's been said, meals are eighteen hundred hours. Learn what that means in military time, or you will starve. That's all for today and there is your tent.'

The three recruits entered the tent, where there were four beds with bed clothes folded on top of each pillow.

Terry spoke first. 'I'm Terry Hay.'

The taller of the other two replied, 'I'm Jake Rooke.'

The last recruit said, 'I'm Ed Smith. It looks like we're in for an education.' They all nodded and began to make their beds. The evening meal was reasonable. They even had a dessert.

Later that day they were kitted out. The quartermaster issued a khaki jacket, breeches, braces, riding boots, a felt hat with a chin strap, a water bottle, a blanket and haversack plus underclothes and some toiletries. A rifle or carbine (a shorter barrelled rifle), a bayonet and a bandoleer for holding rifle clips of ten bullets each, would be issued later.

Next morning arrived with a bugle call at zero six hundred hours. The three recruits were now in the Army! Breakfast was wholesome and plentiful. After breakfast, they assembled ready for their first real day in the army.

Corporal Jones explained how to march, turn, about face and to halt. The troop did this for several hours each day until they were a smart performing team. Many complained within the troop, believing that as Light Horse, they didn't need to march all the time.

Corporal Jones anticipated the query. After two weeks of marching, he said, 'If you're wondering why you are taught marching, it's because all soldiers are taught to march – new officers, doctors, gunners, military police etc. Today will be different; you will have your riding test. Fall in and follow me.'

The area for the test was the size of a football field. In the centre were three hurdles. The first one was made of brush, the second had several horizontal poles and the last was another brush hurdle with a water ditch on the far side. Twenty horses were tied to the fence rails with twenty saddles and bridles on the fence alongside the horses.

This was the truth test – whether they stayed with the Light Horse or were transferred to the infantry, also known as foot sloggers.

The men were required to saddle a horse and then ride two circuits around a fenced area, jump the three hurdles and finally jump the three fences again with their arms folded. Of the twenty men, two failed when their saddle slipped and two fell from their horse at the first brush fence. These four had lied at their interview; they couldn't ride.

Terry did well. He saddled up and rode the horse at a canter for a minute or two. Then dismounted and rechecked his saddle strap was tight. He completed the test successfully until at the last water jump with Terry's arms folded, the horse baulked. Terry turned the horse and walked him to the jump for a look. He then tried again. This time the horse jumped successfully.

The instructor walked over. 'I noticed you ride with long stirrups. Why did you dismount and retighten the belt?'

He replied, 'We always do that when we go mustering.'

'You joined in Melbourne but you're not from the city are you.'

'No, I'm from Mylonga on the Murray River.'

The instructor walked over to Corporal Jones and said, 'He's your best rider by far.'

Next morning, the corporal said, 'Today you will select your horse. There are fifty to pick from. Choose carefully. The horse is yours while you are in the Light Horse.'

Terry took his time and eventually selected a smallish four-year-old mare. She was a Waler, a well-known breed possessing stamina. She had clear eyes, a shiny coat, her hoofs were without cracks, she walked well and evenly, and she was in good condition. She had four white hocks and mane. He decided to name her Mylonga.

'Tomorrow you will spend the day listening to lectures. Pay attention, your life may depend on that advice,' the corporal advised. 'Primarily, they will focus on your survival and your horse's, be it in a jungle, desert or European countryside.'

The lectures were interesting but by mid-afternoon, their attention began to waver. The instructor called it a day and asked for any questions. When none were forthcoming, he dismissed the class.

The next few weeks were spent carrying out field exercises. They even spent one night sleeping out in the rain with cold rations. Only the tea was hot. Mock charges were popular – racing their horses, holding their bayonets forward as a sword and yelling.

An area of several hundred acres had been acquired for a shooting range. Rifles, machine guns, and even cannons were fired there. The troopers soon gained competency and in time they became a formidable force. They were formed into a regiment of some five hundred Light Horsemen.

Orders had been received that they were sailing from Melbourne on the 19th October 1914, only a week away. No leave was granted. A final field exercise was planned for Terry's troop, with another corporal in charge. Corporal Smith was involved in planning and implementing the move to the ship.

The field exercise was to navigate a circular fifty-mile trek. Most men, being from the country, enjoyed these exercises. By mid-afternoon they were heading back to camp – only ten miles to go. The corporal was leading them down a road back to camp when they heard a scream, followed by a loud bang and horses neighing in distress. The troop quickly followed the corporal around a corner.

A hundred yards from the corner was a bridge with the side rails missing. Below that side of the bridge, they could see a four-wheeled wagon on its side in about three feet of water. Two horses thrashed about in panic and a soldier was trapped half under the cart.

When the corporal jumped from his horse, he tripped and stunned himself when his head hit the road. One trooper with some medical experience, said, 'I'll stay with him; you tend to the soldier.'

Terry, 'Yes, you're right.' The horses needed to be freed before they could help the trapped soldier.

Terry dismounted, shouting, 'Someone tend our horses.' Ed and he went to the frightened horses, and he said to Ed, 'Take off your shirt and wrap it around the other horse's head.' Immediately this was done both horses relaxed.

He then yelled to the other troopers to come down and undo the horses' harnesses. This was difficult in the shallow muddy creek, but it was eventually achieved.

The horses were led up and out of the water and tied to a tree. The shirts were then removed from their head. Meanwhile Terry checked to see what the wagon's cargo was. It was bedding and pillows.

Terry had the other onlooking troopers unload the wagon while he talked to the trapped soldier, giving him some comfort. With the wagon almost empty, the troopers slowly lifted the wagon until the soldier was free. It appeared he had been lucky. He was only badly bruised.

When he was asked what happened, he replied, 'A mob of kangaroos came out of the scrub, crossed the road in front of us and startled the horses on the narrow bridge. We hit the bridge side barrier which gave way, and over we went. Thanks to all of you for what you have done.'

Another army wagon came by and took the soldier and the corporal back to camp with the three horses hitched behind. The two wagon horses had a few cuts but walked without limping. The vet officer would check them more thoroughly than the troopers' quick look.

The corporal had a headache, a large bruise on his head and a damaged ego.

When they arrived behind schedule, Corporal Smith came over and asked what happened, and what had delayed them.

Ed replied, 'Ask Trooper Hay.'

Corporal Smith found Terry writing a report of the incident, as he had been asked to write up the incident by the injured corporal and take it to the colonel. He told Corporal Smith the whole story, who nodded and said, 'Well done.'

The next morning, Corporal Smith told Terry to accompany him to the colonel's office. Terry guessed It was about yesterday's incident.

The colonel's outer office was full of soldiers waiting for a briefing for the next day's move to Port Melbourne.

As soon as they arrived, an officer recognised Corporal Smith. 'You two come with me.' He knocked on the colonel's door and entered with them.

The colonel looked up. 'I presume you are Trooper Hay?'

'Yes, sir.'

'Stand at ease. I read your report on the bridge incident, and I think you sold yourself short. I have another report from the injured corporal, and he wrote a very different report. He spoke glowingly of your leadership. I have accepted his report over yours because he is an ex-Age newspaper reporter. I am led to believe you possess leadership qualities. You're an excellent rider, you are educated, and Corporal Smith speaks highly of you.' He continued, 'We leave tomorrow, and we are short a corporal and a trooper suffering severe stomach bugs.

'As of now you are an acting corporal. Normally you would go on a training course, but we don't have time. You will be tutored and mentored by Corporal Smith until he feels you are ready to be confirmed as a corporal. That's all. Good luck. Dismissed.'

They saluted and left his office. Outside the office, Corporal Smith started laughing. 'I enjoyed the look on your face; it was priceless. First, we'll go to the quartermaster's store and collect your stripes and then move you to the corporal's quarters.'

Terry said, 'I'd like to tell Ed and Jake.'

'Yes, do that and then meet me at the store.'

The Light Horse mobilised very quickly and within six hours they had travelled from their barracks by train to Port Melbourne. The troops and horses were soon loaded. The wharf was full of troops and equipment all heading overseas. When they sailed, wives, families and friends were there tearfully wishing them bon voyage. Terry hadn't told his parents he was shipping out. He would write to them.

The squad were told very little of their planned movements to the war, other than they were going to Egypt. Terry had read of the pyramids and the Sphinx during his school days and felt a sense of excitement.

The Indian Ocean voyage was uneventful. The German Raider, "Emden", had been beached at Cocos Island and was no longer a threat to Allied shipping.

After tending their horses, the men daily did exercises to keep themselves fit by running several circuits around the main deck. Rifle and machine gun practice was carried out shooting at a towed target. Most wrote letters each week, even though they had little to write about.

The Arabian coast was a pleasant change of scenery. The town of Aden appeared in the distance. It consisted of small square buildings all sandy coloured. It was not an inviting look. The ship did not stop and continued up the Red Sea to the Suez Canal. Most of the trip through the Suez Canal had the troops up on deck, enjoying looking at the canal scenery. Sometimes a small oasis or a village could be seen in the distance.

Their arrival in Cairo was as chaotic as their departure was in Melbourne. The Light Horse Regiment soon assembled and, after collecting their horses, they rode to their camp. Tents were then erected, and horse lines formed in front of the tents. The camp was near the pyramids and Terry only then realised just how big they were. The pyramids and the Sphinx were enormous compared to statues in Australia.

After establishing the camp, the regiment was given two days' leave. Terry, Ed and Jake became tourists. The first day they wandered around the statues and the pyramids and purchased postcards and scarfs. The next day they visited the bazaars which were dirty and smelled. They each purchased some wooden carvings and a fez, finding the round, square red hat with a black tassel on top, interesting. They were a little suspicious of the bars, although they did eventually find a reasonably clean one and had a few local beers.

The next few months were spent carrying out military exercises. They ranged deep into the sandy countryside and often camped out under the stars. The troopers became fitter, slimmer and impatient to be posted to a battle front.

Their wish soon came true. They embarked a troopship to travel to a place called Gallipoli, without their horses.

As the ship approached the land ahead, they could hear gunfire and the adrenaline began to flow. They began to realise this was the real thing. The sergeant assembled the troops in line, ready to disembark.

A Navy barge came alongside and the sailor in the bow yelled, 'Quickly; on you come.' The barge was soon filled with troops and the helmsman steered away from the ship and headed to the shore. As they approached they could see a narrow beach fronting a small cliff. There were stores laying everywhere and men moving between them. It was organised chaos.

The sailor yelled, 'Get ready to jump when I say and be quick. I don't want to collect a bullet.' The barge slowed and the front ramp was lowered. 'Jump now!'

Terry was in the middle of the barge and when it was his turn to jump, he nearly went under the water.

It was deeper than he expected. With his rifle held high he made his way to the beach and immediately ran towards the shelter of the cliff face. He could hear the zaps overhead of bullets flying around. A sergeant was trying to organise the troops. Several had been hit by rifle fire from the cliff. He could see Ed, but not Jake. The sergeant led the troops up a narrow ravine to a position overlooking the beachhead.

An officer came forward. 'Take your men and defend the hill over there. Don't take your eyes off it. There are Turkish soldiers down there and we don't know how many. Set up a machine gun to cover the track.'

Terry, as the corporal, organised the machine gun placement and arranged his squad into protected positions.

The gunfire continued night and day. Smoke and fumes filled the air. Sleep was difficult for the first week or two, but then they became used to it.

The food was filling, when they managed to get some, but the water was always a risk. Dysentery and typhoid were rife and caused as many hospital cases as the war wounds and injuries. Death seemed to be everywhere. They could see the stretcher bearers working non-stop, bringing back the wounded to the field hospital. Many were transferred to the nearby island of Lemnos for further treatment and recuperation.

The sentry shook Terry awake. 'There's movement below us. You had better come.' The machine gun was loaded, and the troopers were all awake and alert. It was zero five hundred hours. Terry sent a trooper to headquarters to advise the situation.

The first of the Turks came creeping up the gully. Terry waited until about thirty appeared and then ordered, 'Fire.' The machine gun roared into life, mowing the leaders down. The riflemen killed several others. The Turks fired in return, but the damage had been done. They retreated down the gully.

An officer and four troopers ran into Terry's assigned area. He asked, 'Give me a quick report.'

'Well, they came, we shot them, they went, and we have no injuries,' Terry replied.

The officer laughed. 'That's the briefest report I have ever heard. Well done.'

The squad stayed together for several months as the war was at a stalemate, until Terry became ill with typhoid and was shipped to Lemnos. He recovered slowly and stayed to recuperate for over two months. He was sent back to Cairo and was then posted to France to supplement the Australian Contingent.

The ship disembarked the troops at Marseilles. They then travelled by train, north to the battle fields.

The closer they came to the battle front near Verdun, the more destruction they saw – villages demolished, fields pock marked with shell holes and stripped trees destroyed. They wondered what was in store for them. The Light Horsemen were assigned an assortment of duties ranging from couriers to some even guarding prisoners of war. The smell of putrid mud and dead bodies was everywhere.

Terry was assigned to a machine gun crew. They were positioned overlooking a main road. They were on a high hill and had a clear view for two hundred and seventy degrees.

There were two other allied machine gun posts either side of him, spaced two hundred yards apart. Several times a day, a German aircraft would fly over them and not attack. It was assumed to be an observation flight. Two days later they were attacked by aircraft with bombs and a few strafing dives with machine guns firing.

They could see German soldiers in the distance, advancing along the road. An aircraft bomb had landed near the left side machine gun post and injured two of the troops. The other two were uninjured and the gun was undamaged. The German ground troops began firing at the hill, but the machine gunners waited until the Germans were closer The Germans were getting more accurate as the machine gunners opened fire. The front German troops were decimated and yet they kept advancing.

A shell landed on the machine gun crew on their right, killing them instantly. Soon after the two left side gun crew were killed by rifle fire. Terry's machine gun crew kept firing, expecting the inevitable.

Suddenly Terry felt a stabbing pain in his shoulder. He had been hit by a bullet. They were eventually surrounded and called to, in perfect English. 'Surrender immediately or be shot.' Terry and his crew raised their arms. The four of them were now prisoners of war. The officer said, 'I should shoot you. Your gun crews have delayed us by over two hours.'

The officer handed Terry and the gun crew over to several older troops. They were obviously not frontline combat troops. A corporal, who spoke a little English, was in charge. He looked at Terry's shoulder wound and said, 'We will patch it up and stop the bleeding.' He marched them back behind the advancing German troops.

He had a large compound, where he kept prisoners until there were enough of them to warrant a major move of them to a prisoner of war camp.

After four days the corporal came to Terry and in broken English said, 'We have very little food or water. I want you to escape tonight. Go to the woods and turn left and keep walking. There is an army camp about ten miles along that road. I will leave the door and gate open after dark. Don't be afraid. My men know I am doing this. Goodbye and good luck.'

Terry told the others. They were unsure but agreed to the escape plan. Two hours after sunset, they opened the door and walked out of the compound and quickly to the woods. The road was as the corporal had said. They turned left and kept close to the side of the road.

They continued without stopping. They could see lights in the distance but felt it was better to arrive in daylight to avoid being mistaken for Germans. They sat on the side of the road and waited. They could hear voices and wondered who they were until a voice was heard saying, 'That's bonza, mate.' They were Australians. Only an Aussie would use words like those.

Just then a truck drove by them, then stopped and reversed. An Australian voice asked, 'Who are you?' When Terry told him their story. The driver said, 'You're the third lot in three weeks. Jump aboard.'

The four were eventually returned to their regiment. Terry's shoulder wound had become infected, and he was sent to a UK military hospital. After an operation to remove the bullet, he had a month's convalescence and was declared fit for duty. He was posted back to Egypt.

A communique had been issued requesting more Light Horsemen for a major push against the Ottoman Empire in the coming months.

When he arrived in Cairo, he was immediately taken to the base near the pyramids. He was assigned to lead a squad of Light Horsemen and told to select a horse from the herd. The herd consisted of horses whose owners did not return from Gallipoli or who had been posted to Europe.

There were around a hundred horses in two paddocks. Terry sat on a rail and looked for a horse. He saw one who reminded him of Mylonga. Another Waler but gelded. Just as Terry approached him, another Waler trotted by. Terry thought, *No, it couldn't be.* But, yes, it was Mylonga. She was leaner and had an untidy coat and long tail, but she also had four white hocks. Terry needed to see the horse's brand. It was a TH over a Y.

It was Mylonga for sure. After so many months, they were reunited. Although she looked healthy, she had been neglected.

The next day he entered the paddock with a noose and bridle. After trying several times to put the bridle on her, he could only manage to put a noose around Mylonga's neck. He walked her around the paddock while talking softly to her. The next day he was able to fit the bridle and place a saddle cloth on her back. By the end of the week, Terry was able to ride her. She was still fractious but obeyed his urging to walk, trot, canter or gallop. The vet gave her a once over, and then gave her the 'All clear'.

After getting the clearance from the sergeant in charge of the horses, he rode her to the horse line outside a long row of tents. The sergeant recognised the horse. It had been returned by a rifle instructor who had the misfortune to contract VD and had been posted back to Australia.

Field exercises were the order of the day. Week after week, they exercised and drilled. They were soon a formidable fighting force.

The big day was to be a push to Palestine. However, water was a problem. A trooper was issued a gallon a day and a horse needed five gallons a day.

On the 8th April, 1916, an ANZAC mounted division rode to attack Romani. So started the battles to force the Turkish Army to retreat. Several battles were won, and several battles were lost.

Terry was with a hundred Light Horse replacement troops and joined an Australian brigade. Within a month he was in the frontline. He was soon under fire when he and fifty others were subject to an aerial attack from machine guns and some light bombs. After cheekily wagging their wings, the German aircraft headed north back to the Turkish lines. Fortunately, there were no injuries and little damage had been done. But it made them look to the skies more often.

Terry was assigned a routine scouting patrol. When they left the base, the winds were strong. They were advised to be alert as they often quickly became dangerous sandstorms. The morning winds were tolerable, but the early afternoon winds became stronger. In the distance a cloud of sand began to grow and was moving towards them. Terry moved his squad to the shelter of a nearby cliff face. It provided some protection, but the sand was burning their eyes.

Terry told his squad, 'Get your horse to lie down and then cover their eyes. You lay alongside your horse and use a damp cloth to cover you own eyes and mouth when it gets too much. Piss on your eye covering and save your water.'

The strong winds with the sandstorm continued blowing for two long hours. When the wind had slowed sufficiently and the sandstorm had passed, the squad stood up and looked around. The horses were partly covered in sand. When they stood up, they were hardly recognisable with their sandy coats. After shaking sand from their uniforms, the squad headed for base.

When they rode through the base gates, they were cheered. The base was preparing a search party for them. The duty officer asked Terry to fill in a report. Two days later he was told to report to the brigade office. When he arrived, he was taken to the brigadier's office.

'Good morning, corporal. I'm interested to know the way you survived the sandstorm. Where did you learn that survival technique?'

'Well, sir, it was my idea. Horses' eyes need to be protected. Lying down for all of us seemed to be logical and why waste drinking water when you can urinate to wet your cloth.'

The brigadier smiled. 'You're a very smart young man. Well done. I'm thinking of issuing a directive to all battalions advising this survival technique. I'll call it – The Hay Sandstorm Survival Technique.' Terry saluted and returned to his squad.

Terry and his squad had a quiet time for the next three weeks. They were all waiting for the big push north. He had been offered a promotion to sergeant but declined. He wanted to stay with the squad. They were a close-knit team.

His squad was on a routine patrol when it was surprised by a Turkish ambush in a ravine. Terry held the horses as his troopers returned fire with their carbines at the Turks' gun flashes. The Turks quickly took off into the scrub. No troopers were wounded in the engagement. Terry chose not to pursue them and only to report the incident. It taught Terry a lesson – to be more alert of his surroundings in future.

Two days later, the brigade came under fire from artillery shells when heading north along the Sinai coast.

An officer rode up pointing and shouting, 'Scatter and head to the base of that cliff. We'll reassemble there.'

Most of the brigade scattered and reassembled in an orderly manner at the cliff face. Several troopers and horses were injured as they dispersed. The brigade medics stayed to do their best in trying conditions.

An hour later, the medics brought in the wounded. They had buried ten who were killed. It was the first time he had seen a badly injured horse. He rode over and shot it. Surprisingly very few horses panicked.

The British captured Baghdad in May 1917. Now the big push started. Terry could see columns of Light Horsemen stretching back for miles. It was impressive. They rode for hour after hour with little rest. Terry's brigade was heading for Beersheba and its water wells.

On 31st October 1917, a dual attack was carried out on Gaza and Beersheba. The Allies' objective was to capture the needed water wells at Beersheba. They needed the water for the horses to be able to capture Palestine. The Turkish Army thought the Allies' objective was Gaza only.

The Allies captured the hill overlooking Beersheba first, and in the fading light, they attacked the Turkish line.

Terry and his squad had formed part of the platoon that captured the hill and watched as the mass of Light Horsemen charged the Turkish defence line. They then joined them in a rear charge.

On and on, hundreds and hundreds of Horsemen advanced, shouting and waving bayonets. First their horses were walking, then trotting, then cantering and finally galloping. The horsemen, the dust and gunfire were thrilling to see. Then came their turn to charge.

The Turks had killed or wounded many in the charge, but as the Horsemen neared the Turks fortification, the gunfire became less accurate as it appeared the charge had been so quick the Turks had not lowered their gunsights. The Light Horsemen were soon at and over the Turks' barricades. Most were using their bayonets and others using their carbines. Some hand-to-hand fighting occurred when a rider had his horse shot from under him. The fighting was fierce.

Terry was riding fast behind one of his squad when he saw the trooper's horse front legs fold. The horse somersaulted, threw his rider and landed on top of him. Terry could not stop; there were hundreds of charging Horsemen behind him. He jumped the barricades and headed into the town. He sheathed his bayonet and unslung his carbine for action. He saw four Turks running to a corner, carrying a machine gun. He stopped riding and fired several rapid shots at them. He hit two and the others ran into a building. Terry then fired a bullet in the machine gun breech rendering it useless.

He rode into the old town and joined other Light Horsemen. The battle was over. There were casualties, as expected, but the Turks suffered many more and surrendered. The Australian Light Horsemen had captured Beersheba and its water wells.

Both Gaza and Jerusalem were captured by December 1917.

Two Light Horse Divisions and a camel brigade advanced on Amman. On 4th May 1918 they fronted a large Turkish army who suffered many killed and wounded. They then retreated.

The Allies were rested and soon overtook the Turks. One battle was won indirectly by deception. They fooled the Turks regarding the Allies' true location. Some thousands of canvas horses were erected, and dummy camps displayed for the enemy to see.

The Allies captured Megiddo on 16th September. The Australian Mounted Division rode eight hundred kilometres in six weeks to reach Damascus on 1st October and Aleppo on the 26th October 1918. It was called "The Great Ride".

The Light Horse under Lieutenant Colonel Olden were the first brigade to enter Damascus, beating Lawence of Arabia by a matter of hours.

Terry and his squad were ordered to scout inland and return the next day. They were to report any Turkish Army movements.

That evening, as they were settling down for the night, lights appeared in the distance. Terry and three troopers went to investigate. They came across a detachment of about fifty Turkish Lancers, who were also settling down for the night.

Terry surveyed the immediate area and decided to move his camp to a series of hills within five hundred metres of the Turks. The squad had a few hours' sleep and then waited to fire at the Turks when they appeared in the morning. The troopers were all good riflemen. They would move back to the next hill when the Turks started to fire back at them.

They opened fire at the Turks in volleys, which confused them. They were unable to judge the number of guns being fired. They fired two more volleys and then moved back to the next hill and readjusted their gunsights to the new distance. His squad reported they had killed at least ten Turks. The horses were moved out of sight, and the squad waited for the first of the Lancers to appear over the hill. They came over the hill in a line at walking pace. Terry could not believe what he was seeing.

The squad opened fire individually as Lancer after Lancer was shot. When they had only about twenty Lancers alive, they retreated. Terry thought later that the Lancers must have thought he and his squad had left the area. They were totally unprepared for an ambush. Within a minute, the squad had killed thirty Turk Lancers, without loss. They then returned to the base by noon.

When he reported this clash with the enemy to his officer, he considered they may have been a scouting party as well.

The Light Horse Brigade continued to pursue the Turks north. There were now only a few skirmishes. Terry's luck ran out during a rifle engagement. As he was remounting, a bullet struck his right ankle. He fell to the ground still holding onto Mylonga's reins. A trooper came to his aid. Leaving the boot on, he wrapped a field dressing tightly around the boot and helped him to mount Mylonga.

Terry's war was over. The doctor looked at his record. 'You're going home; you have been out here long enough. Your ankle needs to be operated on by a specialist. You will walk again but you may have a limp. An unwelcome souvenir of the war.'

He was concerned about what would happen to Mylonga. He was totally devoted to his horse and was worried he may have to shoot her. He would not leave her to an Arab farmer. The treatment of their animals was appalling.

He approached a local Sheik's guard and asked if the royal family could take her.

At that moment the Sheik's household officer stopped and was listening. He looked at the horse and commented, 'She is a very smart mare. I like her colour and markings. Yes, I'll take her for our stable.'

Terry walked away tearfully, but happy the mare was in good hands.

He sailed with a ship full of service personnel returning home in time for Christmas 1918. The feeling was different to when he sailed to Egypt in 1914. The evenings were entertaining. They had a fiddler, two guitarists, four harmonica players and a bagpiper.

The bagpiper played by himself, his tune carrying across the sea. A few nurses would dance Irish reels and Scottish jigs. Community singing became popular. These gatherings helped to pass the time.

They stopped in Colombo to disembark an Indian brigade and uplift water and fresh food. They only stopped for two days, then headed south non-stop to Melbourne. The voyage had become boring, and several fights had broken out, even between friends.

When they entered Port Phillip Bay, the ship's guardrails were lined with the returning veterans. Some had tears in their eyes, others said nothing, deep in their thoughts. They sailed up the bay in brilliant sunlight under a cloudless sky. It made them feel as if it was a "Welcome to be home" sign.

The docking was quick, and the veterans were soon disembarked. They were disappointed to learn they were required to march through the main streets of Melbourne before being dismissed to be with their kith and kin.

Terry was helped to an ambulance and taken to the new military hospital for an examination of his injured ankle. The prognosis was good. The next day his ankle was operated on. Fortunately, the broken bones were aligned and only the tendon needed attention. Two weeks later he was discharged with his ankle still strapped but he still needed a cane. Sadly, he had missed Christmas.

The Army had contacted his family and advised them when he would arrive.

The family had assembled to greet him. He wasn't the only returning veteran. There were ten others.

The railway station was packed with welcoming relatives, friends and even some onlookers. Hugs and tears were everywhere. Terry's family were there – his mother, father and sister, Jane. His parents had aged but not Jane. She had matured and looked great.

That evening they had a family dinner and chatted about everything and nothing. The war was not discussed. They would leave Terry to raise the topic in his own good time.

Terry was the last one of them to return home. Ida was first, closely followed by Jimmy. They had been at the station to greet Terry and had a brief chat, promising to meet up soon.

On the 30th October 1918, the Ottoman Empire surrendered and a month later, the Germans surrendered on the 11th November 1918.

CHAPTER FOUR

England

The fog had cleared, and Jimmy had his first view of England. It was not what he expected. The sky was dull and overcast and the harbour looked very drab. The wharf area was dotted with several two-storey buildings which were used for cargo storage. The men on the wharf were unsmiling and poorly dressed. The scene was one of abject poverty. Jimmy was disappointed at his first impression, but maybe he needed to keep an open mind.

After the immigration process had been completed, most of the ships' crew immediately went ashore. Jimmy waited until Michael appeared on deck and, together, they collected their luggage and hired a driver and coach to take them to Michael's rooms.

Jimmy was surprised the streets were so narrow. Every corner seemed to have an inn or tavern. The main street was crowded with small markets and shops and plenty of shoppers.

Michael asked, 'Well, what are your first impressions of Plymouth?'

Jimmy smiled. 'It's different to Wylonga but it looks interesting. I'll enjoy being a tourist and I must admit it's good to be ashore.'

'Spoken like a true sailor. I agree. I'll enjoy my shore time. Well, here we are. My home sweet home.' Michael pointed to a small terrace building.

Jimmy thought, *I now have a real address for Jane.*

The shipping company had forwarded several letters from her. Sitting by himself in the sunlight he carefully read her letters in order. He wrote that evening telling her of the last month's events and answered some of her queries regarding countries and sights he had seen. The major information in her letters was advising him that Terry had enlisted! The other letters were shorter than his as she led a quiet life on the farm waiting for him to return. Some Saturday nights she went to town with her parents when a special occasion was celebrated but always returned home with them.

Michael had written to his friend in the aeroplane industry and had received a prompt reply. His friend had written a letter of introduction for Jimmy and provided a name and address for him to contact.

Jimmy wrote a letter with a precis of his experience and studies and addressed it to: Mr C. Sparks – Works Manager – Avro Company, Manchester.

In due course, a return letter arrived, inviting him to an interview. Changing trains several times and journeying up through the English counties was interesting. He saw some of the scenes and buildings he remembered from photographs in his schoolbooks. It was a sunny day, which was a bonus. He had heard that most of the time it was rainy.

Jimmy walked over to the Avro Company gateman and introduced himself. The gateman looked at a board on the wall and nodded. Jimmy's name was written there in chalk. He pointed and said, 'Follow this road to the large white doors and enter. A receptionist will show you the interview waiting room. Good luck, young man. It's a good company to work for. They care for you as an individual. To some you are only a number.'

He was surprised at the numbers of buildings and the size of the large hangars. He had not realized the company was so large.

A smiling lady looked up as he approached her desk.

When he gave her his name she commented, 'Well, you will be the first to be interviewed today. The applicant before you has not arrived! Take a seat and I'll let Mr Sparks, the works manager, know that you are here.'

Nervously looking around the room, he saw photographs of the various airplanes the company had manufactured.

After a few minutes the receptionist came back to him. 'Come with me and I'll introduce you. There are two men who will be interviewing you.'

Jimmy took a deep breath, stood up and followed her down the hallway.

She opened a door and said, 'This is Jimmy Symons, and this is Mr Sparks, the works manager.'

Mr Sparks was tall, straight and looked every inch a professional man. After shaking his hand, he introduced Jimmy to the second man, Mr James, the administration manager. He then motioned Jimmy to be seated. Another man unexpectedly entered. Both Mr Sparks and Mr James stood up.

Mr Sparks spoke first. 'Good morning, sir. To what do we owe this visit? I wasn't expecting you. We're about to do an interview for a mechanics assistant position.'

Jimmy was introduced to the general manager, Sir John Giles.

Sir John replied, 'Good morning. Yes, I'm early for a meeting. If you don't mind, I'll sit in. Keep my finger on the pulse – so to speak.'

Mr Sparks replied, 'You're welcome, sir. Please join us. We normally have three persons on an interview panel, but our hangar manager is still in London.'

Mr Sparks started first and asked him a few questions about Australia and his family, just to relax him. He had several papers in front of him. The first was Jimmy's application letter. 'You say here you have recorded your practical experience and studies for the last six years.'

Jimmy replied, 'My experience as a tradesman at an engineering firm and my certificate, plus as a stoker's assistant on the ship I came on to England, and a log of my aviation studies and kites and flat kite experimental flights I carried out.'

The general manager asked Jimmy to hand him his aviation Log. Each of the interview panel were now reading the contents of his logbooks.

After a few minutes, Sir Giles looked up and asked, 'I find your diagram of the shape of a wing interesting. What influenced your drawing? But first, how would you explain the theory of flight to a lay person?'

Jimmy thought for a few moments. He stood up and picked up his application letter and went to the end of the table. He allowed three quarters of the paper to hang over the end of the table and then, holding the remaining quarter flat on the table, he blew over the quarter paper section in the direction of the three quarters hanging over the edge. The paper lifted almost level with the table. Jimmy explained. 'I know the fast air flowing over the top of the paper reduces its static pressure and the static air pressure below the paper remains the same but is now higher and this pressure pushes the paper up. My drawings are based on the wing shape of the Australian Wedge-tailed Eagle in various stages of flight and, fortunately, I'm blessed with a photographic memory.' He then sat down.

Sir Giles sat thinking for a few seconds. He then nodded and instructed Jimmy, 'Please wait outside for a moment.'

Jimmy left the room feeling most unsure of how the interview went. Five minutes later, Mr James came and invited him back to the interview room.

The general manager asked, 'What do you know of the company?'

Jimmy answered, 'Well it is world renowned for its aeroplane production and its major areas are – development and design, manufacturing, assembly and test and modification.'

The general manager interrupted him. 'Good you know the fundamentals of our operation.' He continued, 'With war now upon us, the company is expanding dramatically. We are now offering cadetships to young enthusiastic men like yourself. Your documented mechanical and aviation knowledge, including your references and coming all the way to England hoping to join a company like ours is highly commendable.'

He paused. 'Therefore, my managers and I are offering you the position as our first cadet. Think about it and let Mr Sharp know of your decision.'

'Sir, I don't need to think about it. Yes, I accept.'

Mr Sparks laughed. 'We thought you would say that.' He stood up. 'Now go with Mr James and he will advise you of our terms of employment. If you have accommodation concerns, we have an officers' barracks, which is hardly used except by visiting pilots. You can have a room there if you wish. It will solve any of your travel concerns. Come and see me tomorrow and we'll go through your cadet training details.'

Jimmy left the room in a daze – unbelievable!

Mr James handed him some papers to read and sign. He barely glanced at them. He was to be paid one pound a week for the first month. This would be increased, subject to performance, by two shillings a month per month and capped at three pounds per month from then on. He was then given a key to a room in the barracks and welcomed to the company.

It was late January 1915 and he had achieved the first part of his career choice – he had obtained employment with a major aeroplane manufacturer!

On his way out, the gateman asked, 'How did the interview go?'

Jimmy's smile told him.

The barrack accommodation was next to one of the large hangars and easy to find. A middle-aged lady was at the doorway and was expecting him. 'I'm Ethel Probert, and I keep the rooms fresh and clean. You will be my first permanent resident. I'll be happy to help you with your washing and make you a pot of tea if you wish. There is a small shop and cafe not far away for food and meals. Now I'll let you settle in. I'll see you tomorrow. No doubt you will have some questions by then.'

The room was immaculate and smelled fresh. A single bed was made up and there was a small table with a reading lamp and two chairs under the window. A large wardrobe and a sink completed the furnishings. The window looked out to the runway. Jimmy lay on the bed to settle his thoughts.

Everything had happened so quickly and indeed so professionally. He had not expected anything like this to happen. He thought, *I must write and let Jane know my good fortune.* He wrote three letters that evening. One to Michael advising him of the day's events. The next letter to the Red Line Shipping Company requesting his mail be forwarded to his new address and the last letter to Jane.

His letter to Jane was a verbatim description of the interview. He remembered nearly every word. How could he forget them? He found it difficult to finish the letter as he had not received a letter from Jane for over a month but hoped the Red Line Company had some to forward to him. He wrote to her, saying he was waiting for her letters and news from home and finished with terms of endearment. He told her he loved her and was missing her and to write to him C/- Engineering Department, Avro Airplane Company, Manchester England

The next morning, he reported to Mr Sparks' office. He was greeted with a cheery 'Good morning. You're on time; I like that. Now straight to business. This wall chart is your work program for the next several months, depending on your performance in each department.'

Jimmy stepped closer and read:

1. *Development and Design – 1 month plus – Be able to draw scale diagram of the internal frames of AVRO 504 fuselage and wings.*
2. *Manufacturing – 1 month plus – Be able to cut fuselage and wing frames for both wings AVRO 504 and dismantle and rebuild an engine.*
3. *Assemble – 6 weeks plus – Assemble an AVRO 504 fuselage and wings complete with fabric coverings, cockpit fit out and install an engine.*

4. *Quality, Test and Modification – No specific time.*
5. *Attend lectures and Air Shows – write reports.*

Mr Sparks added, 'Jimmy, attending lectures and visiting air shows will occur infrequently and during your other task assignments. We believe you have the potential to be able to provide some lateral thinking to the company. Currently, we are looking for new ideas for a new single or twin seater fighter airplane and possibly a multi engine bomber aircraft. There are many evolving theories for the best wing design, but we need facts. At the end of your training, you will be attached to the Quality, Modification and Test team.'

Pausing a moment, he continued, 'This team is basically a "think tank". The senior technical officer, Derek Smythe manages the team, with you as a technical officer to assist him plus his three mechanics. Eric Johnson is the test pilot. He has another test pilot and three ferry pilots to complete his team.' He looked up and handed Jimmy a copy of the Avro 504K Trainer Aircraft Specifications and Performance Details. *[NOTE 3]*

'Even with your youth and practical experience, your technical knowledge is more advanced than most of our technical staff. When aircraft operators have defects occurring with our aircraft or systems, the owner or operator is required to forward a defect notification report to us.

'The test team will decide which department should action the defect and advise a modification as necessary. Their actions will be reviewed by your department prior to the company releasing any modification to aircraft operators. You will be part of that team.'

Jimmy nodded.

'Jimmy, when you join the test team, you will generally be inspecting new aircraft from the assembly hangar and handling defect reports and analysis reports. During your idle times you are to concentrate on wing design. Do your own designs, regardless of other opinions. You have a fresh outlook from looking at your eagle's wings and how it flies. Your two colleagues are aware of your project. The think tank will be formed within the next few months. For the time being keep it confidential. Any questions?'

Jimmy replied, 'Not yet.'

Mr Sparks stood. 'Good. Follow me and I'll take you to meet your fellow workers.'

The design and development team was housed in a small multipurpose building and divided into a dozen offices. The supervisor was introduced as George Smith, a smiling Irishman. Mr Sparks then waved and left.

George invited him into his office. He said, 'I have been advised by Mr Sparks of your training program and I hope you enjoy your time here. Initially I'll put you with our senior draughtsman to show you the basics of scale drawing and then you will be given small tasks to improve your skills. Take your time and ask questions. We all had to start from where you are.'

John Edwards was the senior draughtsman. He was expecting Jimmy and had an office ready for him. John was a Londoner with a strong accent.

After he showed Jimmy his office, they sat down. He said, 'I am aware of your experience, but you will need to be able to, not only read scale drawings, but also to be able to draw them. I'll help you all I can, however the result of your training is up to your aptitude and diligence.' He stopped and handed him a manual titled "The Basics of Mechanical Drawing". 'I want you to study this in depth for the next two days. This is your bible while you are here. We will talk more later. Morning and afternoon tea is brought around, and we have a forty-five minute lunch from midday. I'll introduce you to the others then. I'm looking forward to helping make your time here successful.'

John then left Jimmy sitting at a desk, holding the manual he had given him and thinking of John's words.

He looked around his office. In a corner near the window was a tiltable drawing board with paper rollers at each end and a stool.

A wall mounted shadow board had a collection of rulers, set squares, dividers, compasses, parallelograms, triangles and other items with which he was unfamiliar. Several bottles contained pencils etc. This was his own domain. Jimmy then realized that the company had left it to him to prove his value to them. He decided he would accept any challenge head on and succeed.

The manual consisted of ten chapters. He decided to read it completely before studying it in detail. He found it easy to understand and logical to follow. At the end of each chapter was a scale drawing. Jimmy would be given a task like the example in the manual. The first chapter started with simple drawings as examples to carry out. The manual finished with a three dimensional scale drawing of an engine piston and a piston rod. He knew this would be testing his skills. He spent the first day reading the manual from cover to cover. He felt confident he could measure up to their expectations.

During the first tea break, he was introduced to the others working in the department. They were all middle-aged men and worked quietly at their drawing boards. Friendly but reserved. He was unconcerned as they would not have similar interests, other than the war.

The next morning, he visited the café and had tea and toast before heading to his office. Today, he decided to study each chapter in earnest as he now knew what was required of him by the senior draughtsman.

As he read the first chapter, he decided to draw the first example. He found it easy. He then proceeded to draw the second example. By lunch time on the second day, he had completed the first five examples. He struggled with the examples from chapter five, so he decided to just re-study the next five chapters. After he re-read the last five chapters a second time, back in his barracks room, he felt confident he could answer the senior's questions.

Jimmy was sitting at his desk as the senior walked in.

'Good morning, Jimmy. How did the studying go?'

He replied, 'I found the manual easy to follow and even tried a few test examples. They're on the drawing table for you see.'

John walked over and spent several minutes checking each drawing's scale and layout. He sat down. 'Good. I hoped you would draw some examples without my input. As you know, from now on the challenges are more demanding. I suggest you only try one a day. I don't want you getting frustrated and making mistakes. You have made an excellent start. Keep the bible; it's a present from the company. Remember one chapter per day. Chapters nine and ten will not be easy. You may need more days.'

When the senior left, Jimmy did a jig around his office and then went to the drawing board to tackle example six. He heard an engine running outside his window and being inquisitive, he turned his chair to look out to see an Avro 504 airplane taxiing towards the runway.

He kept looking out as the pilot opened the throttle and sped down the runway and slowly rose into the air to vanish into the distance. He knew he had made the correct career choice. Maybe one day he would learn to fly!

The example in chapter six was difficult. It was a coil spring and Jimmy was unable to get the scale correct. After four attempts he decided to go for a walk and see if any mail had arrived for him. He was in luck. He had two from Jane and one from his father. He would read the letter from home in his office and keep Jane's letters for tonight. When he arrived at his office, he sat at his stool and read chapter six again. What was he doing wrong? He thought on it for a while until it suddenly came to him. It was simple; he was misreading an angle direction. It took him the remainder of the day to complete the drawing to his satisfaction.

That evening, he purchased two hot pies from the café and sat in the late afternoon sun. Jane had numbered her letters. She first told him about the latest gossip in the town. Her father had broken his leg assisting in a rodeo event and was homebound for two months at least. Their shearing had been carried out in dry weather and the wool yield had been better than the family expected. The price per bale was also very good, due to the increased wool demand created by the war.

Jane had purchased a well-bred filly and began to train for local gymkhanas. Together with her father, they had marked out a practice course in the home paddock. She said her social life was quiet, but she felt contented. She missed him terribly and looked forward to his letters.

Her second letter was about how the war had influenced the local population. Many of the young men had joined the army; some were in the Australian Light

Horse. Two others had joined the Navy and had already gone to sea. Jane mentioned names he recognised from his school days.

Jimmy wondered where the war would lead him. He knew he was doing his bit with his involvement in the production of military aircraft. But was it enough? The remainder of Jane's letter concerned their families and the farms.

He finished his pies and, after a cup of tea, went to bed. He would write to Jane tomorrow evening.

Chapter seven's project was relatively easy. He had acquired good basic drawing knowledge by now and had gained confidence. It required that he draw a spur gear. The only difficulty was the scale required. It took him most of the morning to start the drawing after doing the calculations, but he finished it by the end of the day.

The following morning, John walked into his office with a cheery, 'Good morning. I thought I would drop by and check your progress.'

Jimmy nodded. 'I've completed six and seven. They're on the desk for you. I'm starting number eight today.'

John walked to the desk and after a few minutes, he looked up and commented, 'Your progress is as good we had hoped. Keep up the good work.' He turned around and left.

Jimmy read the requirement for number eight twice before picking up a pencil. It was relatively simple but required extensive detail in a small scale. It took over a day to complete. He didn't finish until noon the next day.

Just as he finished, the chief designer walked in and sat down. 'Good morning. How are you progressing? Are you handling the challenges?'

Jimmy answered, 'I read the bible twice before I started. I found it easy to follow. Before each assignment, I read that chapter the night before and, yes, I'm handling the challenges. They are demanding but have logical answers.'

'Your supervisor agrees with your comments and is pleased with your progress, seeing it's a new field for you. Keep up the good work.' He stood up, nodded and left the office.

Assignment number nine was a puzzle from the start. The scale was in metric and imperial, and this confused him further. He was unable to grasp the concept. The drawing was of a tool needed for a specific task. Jimmy was unable to get the angles correct. After wasting all morning trying, he decided to go to assignment ten. The number ten assignment was different. A three-dimensional drawing of a piston and piston rod. It was difficult but he completed it in a day and a half.

John Edwards walked in and, after checking Jimmy's number ten project, he said, 'I've been asked to produce a detailed drawing of the aerodrome, roads etc., and all the buildings, including any other items of interest. I'd like you to do it. You are ahead of your allotted time with your projects, and I think it would be a change for you. What do you think?'

Jimmy nodded. 'Yes, I'd like that assignment.' He knew this would take a week at least. He decided to tell the senior he had skipped test number nine as he was having trouble starting it. He asked if he could complete the aerodrome task before tackling number nine.

John looked at him and said, 'Yes, I knew assignment nine would be difficult. I agree. Do the aerodrome drawing first. It's seriously out of date. It will require you to do some field research. Shirley has the land map and the buildings plans. That will be a good place to start, and I would suggest you allow yourself several days.'

Jimmy nodded and replied, 'Thank you.'

When Jimmy went to see Shirley, she smiled and asked, 'What can I do for you on this sunny day?'

Jim returned her smile. 'I have an assignment to update the plan of the aerodrome and its infrastructure. I believe you can help me. I need any plans or diagrams of the aerodrome, the buildings and any other information you have in your files.'

She replied, 'Come with me. There is an entire drawer on that subject here in this corner. This is it.'

She pointed to a drawer marked "Airfield Dimensions and Buildings Plans".

Thanking her, Jimmy examined them one by one. It took him over an hour to select the ones he was looking for. He had written a list.

1. Aerodrome Council plan.
2. Building 1   Offices and staff facilities.
3. Building 2   Design and Development.
4. Hangar 1   Parts Manufacture.
5. Hangar 2   Aircraft Assembly.
6. Hangar 3   Quality and Test.
7. Building 3   Barracks accommodation.
8. Building 4   Main Guard House.
9. Building 5   Ground equipment Building.
10. Building 6   Security and Beacon lighting
11. Building 7   Guard houses.
12. Building 8 Inflammable and explosives Store.
13. Internal Roads.

He found them all, but discovered the scales were different in several drawings. More work! However, Jimmy was happy to have found all the drawings he needed. Thanking Shirley again, he packed the documents into a box and returned to his office. Looking out his window, he decided he would walk around the aerodrome to see if he needed more information.

The aerodrome was three hundred and fifty feet above sea level and was a rectangle – four miles by two miles. Lengthwise it ran west-east, due to the prevailing winds coming from the west. The entire surface was grass, flat and well drained. It had a ditch about two feet deep, two yards inside the entire perimeter fence. A coloured windsock gave incoming pilots the wind direction. With the size of the aerodrome, they were generally able to land straight into the prevailing wind direction.

A floodlight was situated at each corner of the aerodrome and a flashing beacon was installed midway along the north fence.

During his walk, Jimmy suddenly realised that every building was painted a drab green – sides and roofs. He measured some of the buildings to check their dimensions were as per their drawing. He was pleased to find the buildings were as per their drawings and that their north walls were all aligned in a straight line. He needed to measure the buildings' distance from the perimeter fences as he was unable to find any reference to these figures.

He also noted some small buildings were without a drawing or any reference in the files. They might be only minor, but he would include them in his master plan. The dogs' kennels was one. The security guards used them during their night patrols. Others were the roads and the car park; they had not been added.

After his walk, he was ready to start drawing. He decided on a four-feet by two-feet sized drawing. The paper took up the whole area of his worktable. He began drawing the aerodrome perimeter first and then added the buildings as per his list. Converting the buildings to the scale he had decided on was time consuming and naturally annoying. Jimmy preferred to be drawing rather than doing calculations. After five days, he still had more work to do on the master drawing, but the assignment was coming together. He was pleased with his progress.

That weekend Jimmy travelled to Cheshire. It was like most English towns. History was at nearly every corner. He purchased several souvenirs for Jane and his family and shipped them home with a short note.

During a drink at a small wayside inn, he struck up a conversation with a young army officer who commented, 'I'm here to collect an aircraft and deliver it to a southern airfield.' His name was Martin Mullins. When he found out who Jimmy was, he was delighted to identify with a fellow aviation person. It transpired that he would be staying at the same barracks. After a few more ales and dinner they headed to the aerodrome barracks.

The following morning, over a cup of tea and toast, Jimmy asked, 'What's flying like?'

Martin thought for a moment. 'It can range from utter terror to sheer delight. Some aircraft can be very testing during take-off and landing, but once in the air, it's a different story. If you keep your speed and height up, you're going to survive. As you know, the aircraft are continually developing and are easier and safer to fly. I've only flown twenty hours and I'm still learning.'

Jimmy interrupted, 'I'd like to fly one day and, yes, I agree, aviation is still being developed and will be for many years. One of my future tasks is to design an improved wing design. Designers are concentrating on the engine thrust and the wing lift, but we know very little about drag. It's the third component and is not being explored enough. We need to learn from the large birds who glide.'

Martin nodded. 'Wise words from one so young.'

Later Jimmy waved to Martin as he taxied his aircraft. With the engine roaring, he sped away and lifted off, climbed and headed south. He wondered if they would meet again.

Back at his drawing board, he painstaking added building after building. He sat back and nodded to himself. The master plan was coming together. Just then, in walked the manager and the senior.

'Good morning. We thought we should pop in and say hello. How is the master plan coming along?'

Jimmy stepped back to allow them a closer look at the drawing board. He waited with bated breath.

The manager turned, smiling and said, 'Excellent. Well done. When will it be finished?'

'Two or three days I should think.'

'Keep up the good work. We'll come back in three days. Bye for now.'

Within the next two days, he had finished the master plan to his satisfaction. He spent the previous night checking and rechecking his dimensions and scale. He had even added small details such as the three concrete tie down points used for keeping the tail of an aircraft roped down to stop it tipping forward when testing an engine at full power. He felt sure he had added all the plan details required.

Day three arrived and, true to their word, he was visited by the manager and the senior.

The manager smilingly said, 'The moment of truth has arrived, young man.'

Jimmy said nothing and stood back.

The manager looked carefully at his drawing for several minutes and then turned to him. 'When I first met you, I was unsure about your prospects, but now, I'm sure. Well done. It's excellent. I'm sure the general manager and indeed the board will be impressed. I'll send this to our company marketing team. They can have their colourist enhance it. You have made my day.' As they left, the senior gave him a discrete thumbs up.

Now that the master plan had been completed, Jimmy returned to assignment nine. He spent a morning trying to appreciate the task objective.

Suddenly, he realised that it was a specific, once only task, and he could use his initiative. He could do it his way and not follow the norms. He decided to design his own tool to be used for the task. Within two days he had successfully completed the final drawing.

Shirley, Mr Spark's secretary came to Jimmy's office and advised him he was required to be at his office at eleven hundred hours.

He realized his time in the design and development department had been completed and he was to move on to the manufacturing department. He had enjoyed his time at the D&D and had learnt a lot in a short time. But more challenges were awaiting him.

Mr Sparks invited Jimmy to be seated. He coughed and said, 'I trust you enjoyed your time at the D&D. Your report is excellent. I don't know if you realized but you were deliberately left unsupervised for most of your time there and you came through with flying colours. Tomorrow you will report to Mr Williams, who is the manager of the manufacturing department. We have allowed a month for you to be with them, but that will depend on your progress. That's all for now. Keep up the good work.' He stood up, shook his hand. Jimmy went to the barracks.

The next morning, he was sitting outside the office of Mr Williams. He saw a well-dressed man approaching and stood up.

The man offered his hand. 'You must be Jimmy Symons. Please come in and take a seat.'

He nodded and said, 'Yes, I'm pleased to meet you, Mr Williams.'

'I have read your file and I think you will enjoy working here, particularly with your mechanical experience. You will need to learn woodworking skills, but you can set your own pace. You will work with an experienced carpenter and woodcarver, Bill Long. He will guide you. I'll take you to him now.' They walked into a very large hangar and approached a work bench.

The occupant stood up and was introduced. 'Meet Bill Long, your mentor for the next month or so. I'll leave you in his capable hands.' They shook hands and Mr Williams turned and returned to his office.

Bill said, 'Its near cuppa time. Let's get one and have a chat.'

Jimmy's first impression of Bill was good.

Bill said, 'I know you have mechanical and engine experience, so I suggest we start on developing your woodworking skills. You will like it here. We get on well with each other and, to a certain extent, we socialise out of work hours. First tell me a little of yourself.'

Jimmy spoke for a few minutes, just glossing over his life and his interest in aviation.

Then the whistle sounded, and the workers finished their cuppas and returned to their work stations.

Bill led Jimmy to a long narrow table with painted lines marked on it. He explained that this was a template for a wing rib. Long sections of wood were stacked nearby. Bill told him that the first task in shaping ribs and frames was to inspect the wood for faults – cracks, splits, knots and growth faults. 'We pay particular attention to the wood grain. Come I'll show you.

'Even though it has been inspected by the suppliers, we still reject around five percent of their wood. This is a good example. The grain of this piece of wood has no flaws. This other example shows how the grain is twisted and is not uniform. Here is another piece with small cracks. I'm surprised the supplier didn't notice them. Your training will consist of observing how the wood is cut and shaped.'

Bill went to his desk and handed Jimmy a large volume. 'This is a manual showing all the wooden parts of the aircraft. Rather than giving you a tour today, I think it would be better if you familiarise yourself with pertinent details first. So take the rest of the day to study the manual. You can use the staff canteen and we'll talk tomorrow.'

Jimmy nodded. 'Thank you. I think that's a good idea.'

With the manual under his arm, he found a quiet corner in the canteen and began to read. That evening he read the book again. It took him four hours, but the time was worth the effort.

The next morning Jimmy was given a detailed tour of the hangar workstations.

Bill was most enthusiastic about the workers' performance and on time supply of wings and fuselages to the assembly hangar. He advised that the company had highly experienced quality Inspectors performing independent standards checks of the wood and finished frames and ribs.

Jimmy worked with an experienced wood worker for three weeks. During the fourth week he was required to cut several frames under Bill Long's supervision. He was slow but accurate and, more importantly, he was found "most satisfactory".

The fifth week he was moved to the engine overhaul section. His task was to disassemble an engine waiting for an overhaul. He was to reassemble it, after an assessment of the work required had been decided by an engine specialist, replacing worn parts such as piston rings etc. It was a straightforward task, and he followed the instructions in the engine overhaul manual.

The following Monday, Jimmy accompanied the engine specialist to a steel framed structure onto which the engine was bolted. A propellor was fitted and then they started the engine, after a few attempts. It ran smoothly and had no oil or fuel leaks.

During each of these weeks Jimmy documented all the various tasks he completed. Bill Long was happy with his performance and signed a logbook as his supervisor.

Mr Williams sat reading Jimmy's report of his last five weeks' work in his department. Jimmy sat quietly waiting for him to talk.

Eventually, he looked up and smiled. 'Good. You're progressing very well. The supervisors speak highly of you. I hope you enjoyed your short stay with us and no doubt we'll meet again. Bye for now. Mr Sparks would like you to drop past his office.' He stood up, shook his hand and opened the door for Jimmy.

Mr Sparks invited Jimmy to be seated. 'How are you finding your project? I've had good reports on your progress. The board is very interested in our cadet program. I update them on your performance at our monthly board meetings.'

Jimmy answered, 'I have enjoyed the challenges and I'm learning more every day.'

Mr Sparks nodded. 'Good. The assembly department is much larger and will finish your training. From there you will go to the quality and test department as a technical officer. Mr Ian Jackson is the manager. You will report to him this afternoon. Goodbye and keep up the good work.'

The assembly hangar was much larger than the others. Mr Jackson stood up and greeted him with a cheery, 'Hello and welcome! Come with me and I will show you around. I think this cadetship is a good idea and I hope it works out. Your reports show it is at this moment.'

Mr Jackson said, 'We complete three airplanes per week. We have four work teams. The first group, assemble the upper wings. The next group, assemble the lower wings. The third group, assemble the fuselage, fuel tank and the final group fit the wings to the fuselage, fit out the airplane cockpit, install wheels and skid, the engine and the propellor.

'We also offer an overhaul and repair service for Avro aircraft.

'On Monday mornings, our storemen start two hours before the assembly teams arrive and lay out all the parts and materials for them, in four separate areas.' Mr Jackson pointed them out. 'The four teams have an experienced quality inspector overseeing each assembly process. This includes the joining of the frames, the fitting of the surface material and doping, the installation of the wing wire fittings, struts and the rigging and jigging of the wings being attached to the fuselage and engine installation.

'After the airplane is assembled, it is towed to the quality and test hangar. There is then a final inspection, the wing angles are double-checked, and functional checks are carried out and there is a test run of the engine.' He paused. 'I have assigned you to work with one team only. The first week you will observe and the following week you become an active member of that team. After four weeks we will assess if you are ready to join the quality and test team.'

Mr Jackson called to a workman nearby. 'Jimmy, this is Ian Lane. He will be your supervisor while you're in this department. You're in good hands. He's our most experienced mechanic. Bye for now.'

Ian and Jimmy shook hands.

'Let's have a cup of tea and you can tell me about yourself,' said Ian.

When Jimmy finished, Ian just said, 'You seem to have packed a lifetime into a few years. Let's hope you enjoy this department as part of your life story.' He laughed. 'For the first week you'll be with me to familiarise yourself with the area and work routine.'

For the next week Jimmy followed Ian around the assembly areas. He could see assembly work would become routine after a while. But he knew it would still be possible for a mistake to occur.

He was surprised by the number of women sewing the wing coverings. They were probably better at this skill than men anyhow. Jimmy soon picked up the process of assembly of the frames, then the use of glue and forming of a wing frame. He understood this from his experience in the design department. He gradually realized he knew more about the Avro 504K airplane than most of the Avro staff.

The first week went quickly. He both listened and asked questions. By the week's end he was satisfied he had a good grasp of the way the company operated and its objective to produce an excellent airplane.

The next four weeks were long and somewhat boring. Except for the rigging of the wires, the fuselage and wing assemblies were routine. In some ways it reminded Jimmy of a child's jigsaw puzzle.

The repetition imbedded the steps of assembling the respective tasks in his mind. He even tried his hand at sewing the fuselage skin materials together. The doping mixture they applied over the material gave him a headache.

One woman said, 'After a year you don't notice it.'

Jimmy smiled and thought, *That won't be happening to me!*

The attachment of the wings to the fuselage was easy, only a few bolts were needed and the same with the struts. The rigging of the wires between the wings and fuselage required special attention.

The angles of the wings to the fuselage were crucial to an aircraft's performance and its structural integrity. Even with the diagrams, one needed to concentrate on the complex rigging tasks.

The most interesting jobs he found were the fitting out of the cockpit and installing the engine and its controls. Due to the size of the cockpit only one person could fit into it at a time. Jimmy sat in the cockpit with an experienced mechanic standing alongside him on the wing, instructing him how and what to do. By the time he performed the third fit out, he felt confident he could handle the tasks without supervision.

At the end of the fifth week, Ian Lane said, 'Mr Jackson wants to see you. I think it's good news.'

Jimmy nodded and asked Ian to sign his worklog, which he did and wished him good luck before shaking his hand.

Mr Jackson's office had Mr Sparks and another person in attendance who Jimmy had not met. Mr Sparks said, 'Good morning! Jimmy, have a seat. I read your last report and I see it was another good one. Well done. You have justified our decision to start a cadet scheme. Each report I received on your training progress and performance has justified our choice of you as our first cadet. As from Monday you will join the quality and test department as a technical officer. This is Derek Smythe our senior technical officer. He will be your supervisor.'

Derek nodded and smilingly said, 'Welcome aboard. I'm looking forward to you joining our team.'

Jimmy was expecting this promotion, but he still felt a bit emotional. He had achieved his ambition to be employed in the airplane industry in a matter of months. He couldn't believe how lucky he'd been. Jimmy stood up. He felt he needed to say something. He started, 'I would like to thank you for your confidence and trust in me, to give me this start in this industry. It has been my dream since my school days. Thank you again, Mr Sparks.' The secretary then came in with tea and scones.

That evening Jimmy wrote to Jane, his father, Michael and Ida, telling them of his good news. He wondered how long it would be before he received an answer. He had received some letters, but they seemed to be out of order.

The following Monday, Jimmy reported to Derek's office. Over a cup of tea, Derek explained the objectives of the quality and test department. 'We are only a small but an essential team. We consist of myself, two technical officers and three mechanics. The flight test team comprises a chief test pilot, an assistant test pilot and three ferry pilots.

'We are responsible for the final check of our airplanes before delivery. Initially, you and I will spend a day inspecting each airplane delivered from the assembly hangar. We will then run the engine and function check the controls and instruments. When we are satisfied, our test pilot will do a few taxi trials and then test fly the airplane. All things being satisfactory, we then deliver the aircraft to anywhere in the UK. A secondary task of ours is to evaluate aeroplane defects advised by their operators and decide a course of action to correct the problem.

'Your training was targeted for this technical officer position, as you no doubt realise. Our other technical officer is at an army officers' training school. I don't expect him back.'

That morning Jimmy had his first lesson in engine starting and testing. After having the mechanics place chocks in front of the wheels, they removed the engine cowls and filled the engine with oil. Derek and Jimmy inspected the engine, pipes, hoses and components for security. They then exercised the engine controls for correct movement.

Derek half-filled the fuel tank. He then sat in the pilot's seat and set the throttle and turned the fuel valve to on and checked the magneto switches were set to off.

Jimmy stood on the wing alongside the cockpit and watched. When Derek called to the mechanic, 'Switches off,' the mechanic pulled the propellor to an engine compression stroke. Derek called, 'Switches On,' and the mechanic quickly pulled the propellor around half a turn, moving back quickly to a safe distance.

On the third attempt the engine started, throwing a cloud of exhaust smoke into the air and at Jimmy. The smoke only lasted a few uncomfortable seconds, then cleared. Derek pointed to the oil pressure gauge and gave a thumbs up. He waved Jimmy away from the airplane and for the mechanics to remove the chocks. Derek slowly increased the engine speed. It ran smoothly and Jimmy found the noise thrilling.

Derek then taxied it to the front of the main offices. He closed the throttle and shut the fuel valve. They both inspected the engine for leaks and would check for leaks again tomorrow after the engine had cooled.

The next day they inspected the engine. No leaks! Good. Derek then told Jimmy to sit in the cockpit. The engine run procedure was repeated. The engine fired on the second attempt. Jimmy increased the engine speed to sixteen hundred revolutions per minute, which was the engine speed cruise setting. He was excited to feel the airplane vibrating a little and at the noise of the engine. Derek signalled him to shut down the engine.

The aircraft was to be delivered the next day. Derek and Jimmy went to his office and began collecting documents that needed to be completed for the new owner – The Royal Navy. The most important document was the Certificate of Maintenance Release, which Derek was authorised to sign by the British Civil Aviation Board.

Over the next weeks, Jimmy found he was left to perform his duties unsupervised. Derek still inspected an airplane prior to signing the certification documents, though. Jimmy was now allowed to taxi the airplane but at a walking speed only. He soon became confident and began to wonder if he could learn to fly.

The Avro 504K was a dual seat training airplane. Normally they were ferried with a pilot only.

Jimmy eventually asked Derek if he could go on a delivery flight. 'Yes, why not? Go and ask Eric Johnson. I'm sure he'll agree.'

Eric agreed without hesitation. 'Certainly. Sometimes we ferry airplanes back to here for overhaul or for maintenance. You could give them a safety inspection once over. The ferry flights are listed on the movements board. Take your choice and see the pilot.'

Jimmy's first ferry flight was with John Julian. He was a similar age to Jimmy, and they became friends immediately.

John said, 'Just sit there and don't touch anything.' The flight was to an airbase a hundred miles south. The day was clear and cold. He had been issued with a flying suit, a sheep skin coat and gloves, plus a flying helmet with goggles. The airplane took off into the wind and then turned south. It was only a forty-minute flight, but Jimmy was hooked. He wanted to be a pilot.

He continued to fly as much as he could. He watched every move the pilot made from take-off to landing and how the airplane responded.

However, when they landed at a military base, he was required to remain near the airplane as he was a civilian and had no security pass.

The company pilots were all Reserve British Army officers and had passes. When this issue reached the ears of Sir John Giles, a phone call was made to the Minister of Defence. Subsequently, Jimmy was commissioned a Second Lieutenant Reserve officer in the British Army and required to attend Officers Training School at weekends.

Jimmy continued his everyday responsibilities and to fly as much as possible.

Prior to one memorable flight, John asked Jimmy, 'Do you want to have a fly?'

'Yes, that would be great!'

John said, 'Now listen. When I show a closed fist, you can take the controls and try to fly level. When I show you an open hand, I will take over. Understood?' When the airplane reached an altitude of three thousand feet, John raised a closed fist.

Tentatively, Jimmy took the control stick and placed his feet on the rudder pedals. He gradually began to feel confident. At one stage a gust of wind moved the airplane off course. Jimmy slowly corrected the heading. After ten minutes, John raised an open palm and took over the flying. Each time Jimmy flew with John, he was allowed a bit more latitude and was soon completing a turn to a new heading. Jimmy recorded every flight and manoeuvre he performed, plus flying time.

After several months being taught by John, John had a chat with the chief test pilot. 'When I had Jimmy flying with me, he asked if he could be taught to fly. I have trained him in basic flight manoeuvres and approaches for landing. Would you consider checking the standard he's reached?'

'Yes, why not? He would be an asset to the company. Send him to me.'

Eric Johnson, the chief test pilot, was very experienced and an excellent instructor. Jimmy was unsure why Eric wanted to see him. His fears were allayed when he entered Eric's office, and he was all smiles.

He said, 'I hear you want to be a pilot.'

Jimmy nodded, 'Yes, hopefully one day.'

Eric said, 'Meet me tomorrow at ten hundred hours in your flying kit in front of the hangar and we'll see.'

Jimmy replied, 'Thank you. I'll be there.'

The mechanics had carried out the pre-flight check and fuelled the Avro 504K Trainer, ready for departure. Jimmy was early and nervous. Eric arrived on time and briefed Jimmy, same as John's instructions.

He also said, 'I'll fly about, doing turns and dives. You will then repeat what I've done. We'll then land and debrief. If I'm happy with your skills, we will go up again and do stalls and rolls. Understood?

Jimmy answered, 'Yes, perfectly.'

Eric did the take-off and climbed to two thousand feet and commenced various turns which Jimmy copied. Then came a series of dives and climbs.

Jimmy felt he did quite well.

When they debriefed, Eric pointed out a few mistakes, such as skidding out and slipping in on some turns. He said, 'These faults will be corrected with experience, but generally you have the makings of a good pilot. Now let's go up again. You do the take-off. Let the airplane do its job and lift off first and then you fly it. Be easy on the climb. I'll then take over and perform a stall and show you the recovery technique.'

Jimmy flew the airplane up to three thousand feet, where Eric took over.

He pulled the control stick back until the airplane lost all forward motion and stalled. The airplane went into a spin and continued spinning.

Jimmy was watching the control column and rudder pedals. They were centred and stayed centred until the airplane slowly stopped spinning and Eric gradually pulled back on the control column until the airplane flew level again.

Jimmy had read of this technique in a flight magazine. Eric handed the airplane to Jimmy.

Jimmy pulled back on the control column until the airplane stalled. With the airplane spinning, it was hard to just centre and push the controls and wait for the airplane to stop spinning – but he did! The roll exercise was easy after the stalls. It was done by moving the control column over and holding it there until you were almost horizontal again and then centring it again.

Eric and Jimmy debriefed again.

Eric asked, 'What did you think of your performance?'

Jimmy thought for a minute. 'I was probably a little over-confident and I know that is not a good trait. I'll be a little more reserved in future.'

Eric nodded. 'Yes, you're correct. I'd suggest another ten flight hours may be sufficient hours for your pilot's licence. Keep up the ferry flights with John. He's a very good pilot.'

The next ten flight hours took a month to achieve. Eric was the check pilot and passed Jimmy after two navigation exercises.

Jimmy's progress to become a pilot had been noticed upstairs.

He received a message to report to Mr Sparks office. When he arrived, he saw Sir John Giles was with Him. After greetings all round, tea was served.

Sir Giles spoke, 'Jimmy, we know this war will end one day and we are looking towards that time. What are your intentions for the future? As an Australian I would imagine you will go home one day.' He stopped, waiting for him to answer.

Jimmy replied, 'I have a fiancé in my home town, so yes, I will go home one day.'

Sir Giles continued, 'As you know we have put a lot of time and effort for you to become a technical officer and a ferry pilot. We would hope we have not wasted them. In the future would you consider working for us in Australia as our representative?'

Jimmy immediately answered, 'Most certainly I would. That would suit my future plans, as well.'

With the war intensity increasing, the aircraft were flying more hours and requiring their inspections, sooner. The Avro Company was busier than ever.

Jimmy continued doing inspections in the quality and test department and was doing more hours flying overhauled aircraft back to their base and returning with another requiring an overhaul.

He had been requested to fly to France to deliver an airplane and repair a rudder cable on another grounded airplane and fly it back to base. He and a mechanic were to go.

The flight from the UK was without incident but as they approached the Belgium coast, they could see smoke in the distance and as they flew even closer, they heard the artillery guns firing. The sky was clear and made their navigation to their destination easy.

The airfield was alongside a river. The mechanic had a chart and when they reached the Belgium coast, he saw the river as did Jimmy. He banked the airplane left and flew up the river until the mechanic called, 'There it is.' A small green field appeared dead ahead.

Jimmy flew around the airfield looking for the windsock to see which direction the wind was blowing. Once he saw it, he turned, heading into the wind and landed. As they slowed to a taxiing speed, a motorcycle drove in front of them with a "Follow me" sign attached to the rear mudguard. They stopped in front of a large hangar and were greeted by the duty operations officer.

After handing over the aircraft documents, they were escorted to the mess for tea and sandwiches. The debrief was short and after the tea break, they were taken to the aircraft with the failed cable. A quick inspection showed rub marks. The failure was due to an unapproved ammunition box installed to the fuselage floor rubbing against the cable. It was fortunate that a mechanic had seen the damaged cable.

Jimmy sat in the cockpit and pushed hard on the rudder pedals and the cable snapped. He had saved a pilot and an aircraft from a calamity.

The cable was soon replaced, and a preflight check carried out before they flew back to the UK that afternoon.

Jimmy did several other flights to Belgium and France and accumulated forty five flying hours.

Often when he arrived at a European airfield, he and his mechanic would be sent to drop pamphlets over the battle frontlines. Several times they were chased back by German fighter planes. Twice they found bullet holes in the wings, possibly from rifles fired by German soldiers from their trenches.

The year was 1916 and Christmas had arrived. Uncle Michael was still at sea. Fortunately, Mrs Probert invited him to join her family for Christmas lunch. Although Jimmy was homesick, he enjoyed being with a family. It snowed and snowed without stop. He ended up staying with the family for three days until the snow was cleared from the roads.

VIPs were often visitors to the Avro Works. None more so than Prince Kalifa Bin Ali Arn of an Arab sheikdom. He was young, about Jimmy's age, and was very interested in aviation. He saw the potential it had in his far away land. He planned to stay two weeks and learn what he could in that time.

Sir Giles thought it would be a good idea to introduce Jimmy to him due to their age similarities and Jimmy's all-round aviation knowledge. It was an excellent idea. Kalifa and Jimmy became good friends. He took him into town for lunches and tours of the countryside.

Each day, the two of them walked around the hangars with Jimmy explaining the workings of each department. He even took him on a ferry flight which delighted the young prince. Eventually, the two weeks ended, and the prince was required to go to London to meet with his father. As a parting gift the prince presented Jimmy with a gold ring with the Sheikdom's emblem.

Jimmy presented the prince with a mint Australian gold sovereign, dated 1916.

The years had rolled along, as had the war. The year 1917 was just going to be another of the same, the same and the same again. Except Jimmy was unexpectedly seconded to the Royal Flying Corps – Standards Section. It was not really a surprise as he was a Reserves officer in the new aviation field with special qualifications as a certifying airplane maintenance mechanic and an Avro Company ferry pilot. His orders advised him he had been promoted to First Lieutenant and he was being posted to Egypt.

He was to investigate a recurring problem with a certain Avro aircraft model and to consider the viability of continuing with the limitations of using air cooled engines in the desert climate or replacing them with water cooled engines.

The only information given to him were three reports from pilots who had a major problem taking off and had survived. Their airplanes would dive to the left and if they were not ready for it, they either ground lopped or crashed. No maintenance information was available other than the airplanes had been assembled at this airfield. The Royal Flying Corps regarded this problem as most serious and wanted immediate action from the Avro Company. Pilot fatalities were of major concern, let alone the loss of aircraft.

Jimmy collected all the relevant specification data for the airplane model and had a chat with the chief pilot, seeking his opinion.

He sailed to Egypt on a warship, which was exciting. He was surprised at the discipline instilled in the crew.

They were in the Mediterranean Sea, when the alarm sounded. A submarine had been sighted.

Sailors were running everywhere but within a matter of minutes, they were all at their designated positions. Jimmy had been told to stand at the back of the bridge and to stay there!

The ship increased speed and headed towards where the sighting had been made and released several depth charges when they were over the spot. Their explosions sent large volumes of water twenty feet into the air. The ship performed several figure eight turns and, seeing no disturbance on the sea surface, the ship's captain ordered the helmsman to steer the ship back onto their original course. This happened several times, breaking up the monotony of the long voyage.

The ship docked at Alexandra and Jimmy disembarked and reported to the military harbour master. He was provided with a driver and a car and driven to the local airfield R.F.C. Commanding Officer's headquarters. He was greeted with, 'Welcome. We have been expecting you. Have a seat. I'm Colonel Forbes and this in Captain Edgar. He is across the problem.'

Captain Edgar continued, 'We appear to have a stability problem. We have re-rigged the wings, struts and control cables, time and time again. We have followed the maintenance instructions exactly. We have had different riggers carry out the tasks. Same result. We're at our wits end and we need these aircraft.'

Jimmy said, 'Can we start first thing tomorrow?'

The next day Jimmy had three riggers assist him. First, they rerigged the wings as per their maintenance manual. They pushed the airplane out of the hangar. Jimmy started the engine and taxied to take-off. He slowly opened the throttle to increase his airspeed and slowly lifted the tail. As he did, he felt the airplane tilt. He pulled back the throttle and returned to the hangar.

At the debrief, Jimmy said, 'It's definitely the rigging of the wings causing the problem. I think we had better check the maintenance manual figures. I have the factory manuals and I want to compare the figures in your manuals with my manuals.'

On a chalkboard they made two columns – Egypt manual – UK manual.

As they wrote down the respective figures, all looked good until halfway through the exercise a glaring difference showed. A critical figure for the right wing tilt angle was out by ten degrees.

They rerigged the aircraft to the UK manual's figures.

Jimmy taxied out and repeated the previous exercise. As the tail lifted, the aircraft remained stable as Jimmy continued the take-off. He did three take-offs and landings and taxied back to a cheering squadron. The debrief now needed to discover how this error could have occurred.

The maintenance manuals were not produced in bulk. They were produced as required. It appeared the error was a typing mistake – five instead of fifteen. A simple but deadly error. At least the squadron was now back to full strength.

The current air-cooled engine installation was satisfactory in the colder UK climate, but the desert temperatures were making air-cooled engines overheat and caused their flights to be of a much shorter duration.

Jimmy knew that the engine cowling had baffles which had been installed to retain the air flow around the engine to speed up the warming of the engine and oil and also to reduce cylinder wear. He decided to remove the baffles and allow more air flow over the engine and then carry out some experimental flights. The engines took a little longer to warm, but the extra time taken was of no concern.

Jimmy and another pilot would fly together. Jimmy in an aircraft without baffles installed and the other aircraft with baffles as normal. The two aircraft flew for half an hour and then landed. The pilots then swapped aircraft and repeated the flights. Both agreed that removing the baffles allowed the engines to run cooler for longer. The fix wasn't perfect, but it was definitely an improvement to the aircrafts' operational performance.

Jimmy sent a telegram to Avro and the British Aviation Headquarters, advising the rigging problem was solved, and a temporary fix had been found for the overheating issue and that a detailed report was following. He also requested his next orders. It was four days before he received a response.

'Report to Major Wilson at R.F.C. No. 2 Squadron in Cairo. He will advise further duties.' It was signed. 'Colonel Johns M.C.'

The R.F.C. decided to have all future aircraft fitted with water cooled engines and accepted Jimmy's recommendation for other similar aircraft to remove the baffles when operating in hot climates.

Jimmy packed his bags again. Another change of address and he was off to the Suez Canal. On the seat of a bus travelling to the airfield, he found a British Army newsletter with the headlines – *History created. See page five.* Page five had in large letters. *LATEST AMAZING NEWS – AUSTRALIAN SOLDIER SALUTES A BRITISH OFFICER.* He smiled. Even the Brits had a sense of humour.

CHAPTER FIVE

Gallipoli and France

Ida Whitty had been interested in becoming a nurse. When she completed her schooling in 1912, she made enquires asking what qualifications she needed to become a nurse. The answer was, "Please apply".

Her school grades were above average, she was articulate and presentable. She was nervous before the interview, but soon gained confidence as she realised she was answering the questions easily. She was accepted as a trainee nurse and was sent to The Royal Melbourne Hospital. The hospital had nurses' quarters available if required by country students. This solved Ida's accommodation concern and, also, her parents'.

Ida was eighteen years of age and looking forward to her chosen career and making new friends. It was January 1914. The course was for three or four years depending on the time spent in the classroom lectures and on practical training in either general nursing, theatre operations or emergency and trauma procedures. She decided to do emergency and trauma nursing the first year, theatre the second year and then decide what she would do for her last one or two years.

Her farewell was typical of a country town – friends in the street stopping more often to say hello, invitations to dinner and the expected family farewell dinner.

Jimmy, Jane and Andrew were invited. It was an enjoyable night for all. A few speeches, a few presents.

Jimmy presented her with a writing compendium. 'This will remind you to write.'

The train left on time with her well-wishers waving, crying or some standing quietly. The train trip gave Ida time to think, *What have I done? I hope it was the right decision.*

The accommodation was sparse but warm and very clean. The meals boring but wholesome. Fruit was plentiful. A former grateful patient who had an orchard brought in a variety of fresh fruit most weeks for the nurses.

The other girls were from the Victorian country and southern NSW border towns and were all friendly. Ida soon made friends.

She had promised her mother she would come home once a month if she was allowed. She knew she would be required to work some weekends.

Ida enjoyed the training and even though the trauma cases were difficult to accept at first, she didn't complain.

Which was to stand her in good stead as the senior nurses were watching how new nurses handled major injuries. Her grades were good; not exceptional but good.

The first year was passing quickly. Her grades in the classroom had improved and her reports on her performance in emergency and trauma was graded as very good.

As she promised her mother, she went home frequently and met with her school day friends.

On a sunny day, a picnic was often enjoyed by the four of them on the riverbank in the shade of the tall willows with a basket of fresh salad, fruit and a few beers or ginger beer drinks. They would sit there chatting about everything and nothing. Just friends enjoying a day out together.

One Saturday afternoon they were travelling to town in a two-horse coach from Jimmy's farm, when they came upon an injured rider lying on the side of the road. He said his horse had thrown him and stood on his right knee. Ida could see the knee was displaced and he also had a severe cut on his thigh, seen through his torn jodhpurs. His horse was missing and had probably headed home. After a quick look, they helped him into their coach and took him to the hospital.

The emergency room was empty. However, a nurse soon appeared. After seeing the man's injuries, she went to find the duty doctor. They sat and waited for ten minutes for his arrival. By this time the nurse had cleaned the injured man's wounds.

When he arrived, he quickly decided an operation was necessary to repair the knee. He suspected several ligaments had been badly damaged. He asked the nurse to get a theatre nurse to come in urgently.

The nurse replied both were away for the weekend.

When Ida heard this, she told the doctor that she was a student at the Royal Melbourne Hospital, and she had just completed nearly a year's practise in theatre operations.

The doctor said, 'Good. I'd be obliged if you could assist me in repairing this knee. You probably have more experience than the local theatre nurses anyhow.'

Ida told her friends she had volunteered to assist the doctor in the operation and not to wait for her.

The country hospital theatre room was small but functional. They quickly prepared for the operation, laying out the implements required, including needles, thread and swabs. The ether soon had the patient in a deep sleep. His jodhpurs were cut from the injured leg and the leg was then washed with a strong antiseptic solution. The doctor was quick; his incisions were accurate. Ida had seen similar operations before.

Her role was to hand the doctor the correct instruments when requested. The incisions revealed two separated ligaments and two with slight damage.

When he was finishing the repairs to the ligaments he asked Ida to sew the gash edges together.

She had done this several times before and she carried it out methodically and neatly.

The doctor looked it over. 'You are very competent. Well done.'

Ida then dressed the gash wound and helped the doctor immobilise the knee. They waited until the patient awoke. They then enjoyed a cup of tea. The doctor drove her home.

Ida was unaware the injured rider was William Joyce the son of a very wealthy landowner. It was soon known around town of his injury and a Melbourne Hospital local nurse assisting during his operation. It even reached the Melbourne papers.

Jimmy, Jane and Andrew came around the next morning wanting to know all about her role in the operation. This was to be the last occasion she would see Jimmy for a few years. He left for Europe the following week.

The news of the war in Europe being declared on 4th August 1914 was disturbing. Within a month some Royal Melbourne Hospital doctors had already been called up by the Australian Army. Mainly they were veterans of the Boer War or serving local militia officers.

Ida had nearly completed over two years' training and had decided to continue her emergency and trauma nursing skills training for her final year. She was transferred to her local hospital for three months for further experience. A week later a notice appeared on the tearoom board asking for volunteers to join the Australian Army Nursing Service.

She was still single and had no other ties. She and a friend applied. When her friend was not accepted, Ida lost interest until she was interviewed successfully. The AANS mainly wanted nurses with emergency and trauma training. As she had completed a year's training in that field and was currently in her first year of theatre, that was accepted. Her friend had three years only in general nursing training. Ida found out later only two other applicants were accepted. They had similar training qualifications to her trauma and theatre experience.

Ida signed on in June 1915 and was not queried about her age. She was then sent to Broadmeadows for general military training – marching, saluting etc. for three weeks and two weeks instruction on army medical procedures.

She was then drafted to sail to Egypt on 30th July and was given a week pre-embarkation leave.

She was the only female in Mylonga who had joined the Australian Nursing Medical Corp. She had several invitations to lunch or dinner.

School friends, family and others came to bid them goodbye at the station, which was decorated with red, white and blue streamers. After many kisses and a few tearful goodbyes, Ida, four soldiers and a sailor waved goodbye to their kith and kin, heading to their military destinies.

Ida reported to the Melbourne Military Railway Transport Office for her travel warrant and then met her group to travel to Port Melbourne pier. The group was made up of three doctors, three matrons and ten nurses. She found out later that they were all skilled trauma and theatre medics.

At Port Melbourne she saw a warship for the first time. It was impressive with its grey colour and large guns at the front and at the back of the above deck structure. However, she was more surprised when the group was informed they would be sailing aboard her to Egypt in two days.

Accommodation had been agreed before their arrival. The three doctors and the matrons had been allocated officer's cabins. The absent officers were in the UK, training. One of the four petty officer's quarters had been vacated for the ten nurses. They soon settled into their accommodation and were able to wander around the ship freely.

The nurses were thrilled about being transported on a warship. It was indescribable. They watched the sailors load food and ammunition.

Ida hoped she wouldn't see the ammunition used. The meals were good and wholesome.

Departure day arrived and they were required to be in uniform and assemble on deck, lined up with the sailors. The wharf was lined with relatives and well-wishers, waving as the ship slowly got under way. An Army band was playing, "Wish me luck as you wave me goodbye", to give further feeling to the occasion.

The Melbourne skyline soon vanished into the distance. The nurses felt the ship's movement up and down and sometimes rolling. It was gentle in Port Phillip Bay, but they wondered what it would be like in the open seas.

When they entered the heads, they experienced some rough seas for around thirty minutes. Fortunately for them, today Bass Strait had only choppy seas. They were not rough yet!

The next few weeks were spent listening to lectures from the doctors and matrons. They were also encouraged to give a presentation of some of their exploits.

Ida spoke on the event of finding the injured rider.

The group found this tale very interesting, and she was asked several questions relating to injuries encountered in the country. Most of the group were city born and bred. Ida spoke of gunshot wounds, farm machine major lacerations and even amputations. One doctor commented, 'Sounds like you have already been in a war zone.'

The trip through the Great Australian Bight was rough with westerly winds gusting for four days. Ida's bunk was in the centre and amidship. She slept very well but was seasick twice after lunch. Others in her group fared worse and suffered every day until they changed course and headed north-north-west into the Indian Ocean.

Two days later the ship's captain conducted an emergency evacuation exercise. It was conducted like a well-oiled machine. The crew knew exactly what their roles were. The lifeboats were away, filled with their designated crew and passengers. The medics were conducted to their respective boats, lowered and then rowed from the ship.

Sitting in a lifeboat and looking up at the ship, Ida felt very small.

Within an hour, all boats had been retrieved and secured. The group agreed it was exciting but hoped they would not have to evacuate for real.

The Indian Ocean had moderate seas all the way to Aden. During the journey, some sailors managed to catch fish for the galley. Dolphins often appeared from nowhere and dived and darted about the bow. Sometimes a school of small flying fish were spotted jumping the waves. The lonely albatross would glide over the ship for an hour or so, then head off. One could only guess where to.

A week before they arrived at Aden, the captain conducted gunnery practice. Alarms sounded, accompanied by the Tannoy speaker announcements, creating a feeling of excitement. The group were instructed about the importance of closing hatches and doors. 'Z doors must be always closed behind you with X and Y doors to be closed when advised "In action".'

The group were ushered into a large cabin below the bridge. There were ample windows for them to see the forward guns fire and also hear the directions from the bridge through a large open voice tube. The gunnery office set the pace, ordering crews to standby, loading and, eventually, firing the guns, when the order "Fire" was given. The noise and smoke emanating from the gun barrels was astounding to the group.

After several single firings, a salvo was fired – all guns fired at once. A memory not to be forgotten. The order "All clear" was eventually given and the ship slowly returned to normal.

Aden was a sleepy Arab town at the entrance to the Red Sea. The ship uplifted fuel and some food stocks and sailed within eight hours. When they reached the lakes, they were given priority and sailed non-stop to Cairo. When the Cairo locals realised it was an Australian ship, they were greeted from the shore with calls of "Ned Kelly bastards".

A week before an Australian ship had used a fire hose on the souvenir sellers' bumboats. The bumboats would not move away from the ship's ladder and were blocking access to and from the ship. After being asked several times to move, the ship's bosun turned a water hose on them, causing them to spill their souvenirs into the harbour. The Arabs were most unimpressed.

After a short stopover for a mail exchange and a visit from the Australian Ambassador to Egypt, they up anchor and sailed to the Egyptian port of Alexandra in the Mediterranean Sea to enable the group to join a hospital ship.

The ship's crew enjoyed some time ashore for the first time in eight weeks. A large fleet of transport ships was gathering there to sail to Gallipoli within days.

The medical group was assembled to thank the ship's captain and his crew for their courtesy during the voyage. A few salutes and the group disembarked and were transported to the nearby hospital ship. A new day was dawning. An officer and a matron showed the group to their new quarters, advising them they would meet the next day for a briefing of their respective duties.

The meeting did not get off to a good start. The ship's matron spoke first advising the ten nurses they would be assigned general duties and handed each of them a roster.

The team leader and senior Australian doctor, Lieutenant Colonel Keenan stood up and asked, 'Excuse me, Matron, have you read the qualifications of these ten nurses?'

The matron, replied. 'No, I will in time; nurses are nurses. I'm the matron on this ship and I make the decisions as to which nurse serves where.'

The doctor looked at the faces of the nurses, then got up. 'Matron, you are very much mistaken.' He then left the cabin.

The matron continued, 'I have sufficient skilled nurses already. Dismissed.' The Australian medics were already leaving the cabin, including the remaining two doctors and three matrons. The matron stood there, stunned, and went red in the face with the obvious snub of her authority.

An English doctor said. 'I don't think you handled that very well. You might be the ship's matron, but you just lost the Australian medics.'

The senior doctor who left first went to find the chief doctor aboard. He knocked on his door and entered.

The doctor stood up saying, 'I've been expecting you. Good to see you again. It's been a long time, Noel.'

Noel answered, 'Yes Miles, over ten years ago.'

'How are you settling in?' asked Miles.

'Well, I don't wish to complain, but your matron has caused a problem already.' He continued. 'She had already earmarked the nurses for general duties without reading their files. These ten nurses are very highly qualified theatre and trauma nurses and should be respected as such.'

Miles called out, 'Corporal, please get me the files on the ten Australian nurses, now!' While the two friends waited, they recalled their days in the Boer War, when they were young lieutenants. Miles was now a colonel and Noel a lieutenant colonel.

Within ten minutes Miles had the files on his desk. After getting tea for Noel, he quickly read the files. He called the corporal, 'Get the matron here now and Lieutenant Colonel Keenan will come and see me this afternoon, after I get to the bottom of how this was handled.'

The ship's matron knew something was up when she entered the chief medical officer's cabin, and saw her divisional doctor was there.

Miles asked her to be seated. 'Matron, what can you tell me about the Australian medics?'

She answered, 'Well they are insubordinate.'

Miles interrupted. 'No, I mean their qualifications. What are they?'

'I haven't had time to read their records,' was her answer.

Miles said, 'I believe that you have already assigned them general duties. You should have known this group is a specialized theatre and trauma team. Why didn't you read their records first? You were aware they were coming aboard.'

The matron stood silently, said nothing. She realised she had made a very bad mistake. Her reputation would be in tatters when this got around the ship. After a few seconds, she spoke up. 'I will look into the matter and review their rosters and duties, sir.'

Her divisional officer angerly ordered, 'And do it quickly.'

The matron left the cabin, fuming.

The Australian nurses accepted their rosters and reported for general duty. The wards were quiet. The only soldiers in the wards were sick; none were war injured.

Ida was attending to a soldier with a severe stomach upset and handing him his medicine when the ship's matron rushed past and bumped into her, making her fall to the deck, spilling the medicine.

The matron looked back. 'Watch where you're going next time' and continued walking. Ida was angry but said nothing and put the incident behind her.

Two days later she was called to the lieutenant colonel's office. 'A patient has bought to my attention that the matron and you were involved in an incident.'

Ida said, 'It was nothing, sir. I'd prefer this matter goes no further.' That should have been the end of the matter.

The colonel's aide asked Noel to join him in his cabin. On entering, he saw the matron standing by the colonel's desk. 'Good morning. The matron has written a letter of complaint regarding Nurse Ida Whitty alleging she deliberately pushed her, nearly causing her to fall. Have you any acknowledge of this incident.'

Noel answered by handing over a letter. 'Yes, I have.'

The matron said, 'No doubt it's a complaint letter from her against me.'

After a quick read, the colonel nodded. 'Yes, you are correct. It is a letter of complaint against you, but not by Nurse Whitty. It's from a patient who saw the incident. He further states, 'Whilst the matron was in a bad mood and angry, I believe the push was a spur of the moment thing, perhaps frustration without preconceived malice.'

The colonel looked up. 'Well, Matron, what happens now? The incident already appears to be the talk of the ship's medical staff.' He paused. 'This meeting is confidential but how do we save your reputation? Have you told anyone you have written a letter blaming Nurse Whitty?'

She nodded. 'Yes, I may have.' She thought for a second or so, then said, 'In hindsight, I believe, I should write a letter of apology to her and also give her a personal apology in front of her colleagues. Hopefully that will save the day.' Both officers nodded in agreement. The meeting was over.

Good as her word, the matron did write a formal apology and personally apologised to Ida in front of the Australian team. All was forgiven and almost forgotten.

Three days later the transport fleet sailed to Gallipoli, accompanied by several warships. The hospital ship sailed the following day. As they approached the land mass, they heard the familiar sounds of Navy ships' guns firing at the shore. They anchored behind the transport ships, out of reach of the Turkish shore guns. Within two hours of anchoring, wounded soldiers were coming on board. The ship had three dual theatres.

The Australian team would work together performing a twenty-four hour coverage in the theatre. They would function as three teams – a doctor, a matron and three nurses with a spare nurse to fill in where needed.

Within three weeks the ship was full of mainly wounded soldiers, a few were ill, and some were mental cases. These were due to shell shock of explosions or nearly being buried alive.

The shore gun battles seemed to continue forever, as did the number of injuries. The medicos slept when and where they could. Initially, they handled the terrible injuries with professional aplomb, but with little sleep and non-stop victims arriving, they were all slowly worn down over the months.

The colonel was aware of this and arranged a seven day relief team to come in and give them shore leave. They went to Alexandra and slept, sun-bathed and toured. Within the week they were all fighting fit again.

During her week's leave, Ida met a French sailor – Maurice De Bois – and spent some time seeing the sights with him. She enjoyed having a new friend and promised to write to him.

The war continued in this little area of the world with neither side winning nor even looking like winning.

In September 1915, the first Australian Army wounded returned home. In December 1915 thousands of troops were evacuated without loss of life – an amazing feat of military leadership.

At this time the Australian medical team was transferred to the UK to a hospital which handled theatre cases requiring specialist repair to skeletal and soft tissue injuries. After several months training in new medical procedures and techniques, they learnt they were to be sent to casualty hospitals in France.

The new skills the team learnt, required several weeks of attending lectures in handling soldiers who had been gassed, had burns, suffered shell shock or who had endured a short time completely buried. The lecturing was quick and detailed. Handouts were supplied for out of hours reading.

They then spent a few weeks attending specialist doctor's hospital rounds when he visited burns, gas and mental wards, listening to his questions, the patients' answers and the doctor's decisions. This knowledge would enable a field hospital team to quickly diagnose who should go to the UK or who should not go. It would help clear any bottle necks at field hospitals during heavy fighting.

However, the main reason they were at the hospital was to learn new handling techniques for skeletal and soft tissue injuries. Most of those days were spent in operating theatres and the team performed operations under supervision of a specialist doctor.

Initially they found the work demanding but eventually they all gained confidence in their tasks, whether they were a doctor, a matron or a nurse. After three months they were transferred to an Australian Army brigade in France.

Ida had written several letters to her parents, Jane, Andrew and Jimmy. The answering letters were spasmodic. Now she was in England, she hoped to locate and even meet up with Jimmy. She wrote to him and was delighted to receive an answer within a week. Yes, Jimmy knew where the hospital was. It was near an airfield he often flew to, delivering aircraft. He would telegram her when he was next coming down her way.

During Ida's time in England, she met with Jimmy several times.

As promised, he sent a telegram advising her he would be flying in the next Saturday. He suggested they meet at the airfield mess at eleven hundred hours. She knew where this was and advised her matron of her wish to be off the roster for that day. Her request was granted.

She pondered how long it had been since they last met. It must have been nearly eighteen months or more. She arrived early and sat at the large mess window with a cup of tea. It was a small grass airfield with few buildings, mainly barracks for soldiers, and a few aircraft hangars. One aircraft was taking off and landing again and again. Soon a second aircraft appeared and followed this aircraft, landed and taxied to the area in front of the mess.

Ida recognised Jimmy in the rear seat even with his flying helmet and goggles on his head.

Jimmy left the aircraft and walked towards the mess, obviously looking for someone. The two school friends hugged each other, Ida with tears. They sat down and started to cross talk.

Jimmy said, 'You go first. I know you are an Army nurse but not much else.'

They talked for over an hour non-stop until Jimmy looked at his watch and said, 'I'm sorry. I have to attend a meeting and then I fly out in around half an hour. I'll have to go but I fly into here several times a month. We will meet again.'

They stood up, kissed as friends and he left. Ida sat there with another cup of tea, thinking of what her other school friends might be doing now.

Jimmy walked to another aircraft. He and the pilot climbed aboard, started the engine and flew back to their base. For the first time since he left home, Jimmy felt homesick.

The Australian Army had disembarked at Cairo to commence training and field exercises in preparation for their move to France.

The brigade the Australian medical team was to join had arrived in France in April 1916 from Egypt and were assembling to move north into the Belgium area.

The medical team embarked at Portsmouth and sailed by night to the port of Calais. They were met by a major who had arranged two motorised ambulances to transport them to the brigade's headquarters.

An orderly greeted them and escorted them to a tent signed "Brigade Headquarters". A colonel came over and introduced himself as Colonel Redmond. 'Good to see you here. I'm very busy, so I will be brief. Your role is to provide medical support to the brigade. We intend to have you operate one of several casualty clearance stations based around a half a mile to a mile from the front line, which will be your domain. Several medical first aid posts will be at the front line. They will send the wounded soldiers requiring specialist attention back to you, and they will treat the lesser injuries at the aid post.

'I have had glowing reports of your performance and will chat with you all in due course. However, in three days, we will be launching an attack and advancing to push the Germans back. The casualty clearance station hospitals are already erected and can be moved easily.

Bye for now, my adjutant will show you to your casualty clearance station and your quarters.'

The casualty clearance stations were large tents, each with multiple bed length benches and some beds. Electrical power was available from small generators as needed. Medical supplies and equipment seemed adequate and were stored neatly. Empty boxes were adjacent each bench for soiled linen etc., and sheets and towels were placed neatly on the benches.

A sergeant approached and said, 'I'm in charge of the orderlies and I hope we have set up the casualty hospital correctly.'

Lieutenant Colonel Noel Keenan nodded. 'Yes. Have any of your orderlies been trained in assisting in theatre work?'

The sergeant replied, 'Yes. Ten of us were trained at St Michael's in London.'

'That's good to hear. We will meet all of you over time. Thank you.' The orderly saluted and left.

Their sleeping quarters were large tents with folded beds and canvas shelving for a person's clothing etc. The tents were clean with some flooring. Officers shared with other officers.

The matrons shared with female sergeants. The nurses were in a ten-person tent, so they remained together. Showers and toilets were definitely "field class". They soon learnt not to be late for meals. Apart from the meal being cold, they sometimes ran out of food!

The nurses were surprised and became frustrated to find that they had no authority over the orderlies.

The orderlies completely ignored them and caused the nurses to perform menial tasks when they could have been performing nursing duties. The Australian Military soon recognised this intolerable situation.

The Australian nurses held no rank, hence no

authority. In mid-1916, this situation changed when the nurses were given commissioned ranks.

The big day arrived. At zero six hundred hours a salvo of heavy guns blasted the German lines for at least twenty minutes. Then a bugle sounded, and they heard the soldiers shouting as they charged the enemy lines.

The team had a small casualty hospital with limited staff numbers – three doctors, three matrons and ten theatre nurses and a few trained orderlies. They supported several other casualty hospitals and supplied medical aid to a brigade of soldiers.

By midday, the first seriously wounded soldiers started to arrive, carried on a donkey or a two-man stretcher. The injuries were mainly bullet wounds or shrapnel from hand grenades. Most injuries required surgery to repair the torn flesh or to reset bones. Soldiers with injuries requiring a short recovery time were sent to Lemnos or Cairo. Those needing a long recovery were sent to the UK or home to Australia, particularly if they had lost a limb or had shell shock.

The war raged on, literally bogged down in the mud and mire. The battle of Fromelles and the Somme raged for several months in late 1916. The casualties were enormous. The team gradually began to accept the deaths and injuries as normal. From July until November 1917 the battle at Ypres was fought again with unbelievable losses, mainly at Passchendaele.

Every few months they were given leave in Cairo. Once they went to London. These leave periods were welcome, but the memories of the carnage were always at the back of their minds. Ida had difficulty sleeping because of it.

Ida met Jimmy once more, when he was flying missions over Belgium dropping propaganda leaflets. He was now a qualified pilot and had amassed over fifty hours flying time.

When not flying over German positions, he was delivering aircraft to RAF squadrons and returning with aircraft due for overhaul.

That meeting was to be the last time they would meet overseas. Jimmy was to be posted to Egypt in a special aviation role. They both received mail regularly now. It helped to remind them they were remembered. They shared a film and dinner and sadly said goodbye and looked forward to meeting again.

Ida was still writing to Maurice De Bois. He was at sea but could not say where due to the war. He had been on leave in London twice, but they missed meeting each other. Ida didn't expect to see him again; they were only friends. Ida had been away from home now for over three years and was very homesick.

One of the team nurses came into the tent one day and said she had heard that they were all being posted back to Australia within a month.

Ida was excited but did not get her hopes up. This had happened before, and nothing had happened.

The year 1918 was to see a dramatic change in the direction of the war. The Americans had arrived and, together with the rest of the Allies, began to push the Germans back. The Australians incurred heavy defeats on the Germans at Villiers, Bretonneux, Amiens and Hamel. Hamel was the first battle that aircraft and tanks supported the infantry. The Australian's defeated the German's in one and a half hours. It was the beginning of the end of WW1.

Lieutenant Colonel Keenan called the team together. 'I believe you have heard. We are all being posted to Melbourne. We should be home by Christmas.' He stopped and looked at the team before continuing. 'Well, it's true. We leave in two weeks for London, then home we go.'

Tears, handshakes and hugs were the order of the day. Ida even kissed the colonel. That evening, the team wrote letters to their families and friends telling them of their good news.

Their replacement team arrived within the week and after a stock check and handover of medicines and equipment, the team departed the battle front. They had a week off in France. The brigade colonel arranged transport for them to go via Paris and do some sightseeing en route to Calais.

When they arrived in Calais, they embarked on a troop ship en route to Cairo. They would not be going to London.

After they sailed from Calais, the weather was forecast as storms and rough seas. Sailing through the notorious turbulent Bay of Biscay was very uncomfortable, as expected. It was difficult standing, let alone trying to walk.

The waves were choppy and swirling and throwing the ship around in the seas. Most stayed in their bunks and read or tried to sleep. They skipped meals.

An "All ships" radio message came through, asking for medical assistance. A ship was disabled and was waiting for a tugboat.

A sailor had been badly burnt by an exploding emergency flare and he had fallen and broken his arm in several places.

The ship's captain advised, 'We can help if you can bring the injured sailor to my ship.'

The captain of the ship with the injured sailor replied, 'Yes, we will come to your sheltered lee side, out of the wind. The injured sailor will be strapped in a wire cage stretcher with a centre eyelet on the top. We will be launching a motorboat in ten minutes. Can you keep a spotlight shining on our boat?'

'Yes, we will do that and please keep in radio contact.'

Ida and some of her friends were watching the motorboat approaching their ship. The boat was being thrown about but the helmsman managed to keep it heading to their ship in the glare of the spotlight. When it reached the ship's side, a cable with a hook attached was lowered from a winch. As soon as the boat was alongside and on a rising wave, a sailor connected the hook to the eyelet.

The winch operator immediately raised the stretcher to the main deck. Four sailors carried it to the sickbay, where a doctor and three nurses were waiting.

The spotlight remained on until the motorboat was raised up and onto the other ship. The seamanship shown by the boat's helmsman was first class.

The doctor and his team soon had the injured sailor comfortable. His burns required attention, but they were not critical. His broken arm was placed in a cast. It was a simple fracture and would be healed within two months. He remained on the ship and would be disembarked in Cairo.

After leaving the Bay of Biscay, the ship soon reached Gibraltar. A majestic rock at the entry to the Mediterranean Sea fortified by the British Military. They continued sailing non-stop to Cairo.

German submarines were no longer a threat to shipping. When they reached Cairo, they were advised they would sail again in three days. Ida and some friends took the opportunity to visit the pyramids and the Sphinx. This was one good thing about the war – you travelled and saw sights you would probably never have seen. As usual, Cairo was a hive of activity.

The wharf had loads of military cargo being returned to Australia. Returning troops were also being embarked. Most were due to medical reasons – wounds and mental problems and some were amputees.

The ship's captain asked Lt Colonel Keenan if his team would monitor them. To which he readily agreed.

Sailing day was chaotic. Somehow all the cargo was loaded, the troops embarked and supplies stowed. The ship managed to sail on time. They entered the Suez Canal mid-afternoon and, within a few hours, were enjoying the sunset with its magnificent red and yellow colours. The ship slowly sailed to Ismailia and the lakes. They waited for a day and then headed further south to Port Said and then into the Red Sea.

The medical team had very little trouble looking after the troops. The only concerns were the shell shocked patients. Most just sat quietly while a few others were watched by armed troopers. Only one or two were inclined to be violent. One was even handcuffed after an incident involving Ida.

The patient was mumbling to himself when an armed trooper jokingly said, 'I hope you're getting the right answers' and turned away.

The patient attacked the trooper and punched him in the neck. The trooper collapsed, unconscious, onto the deck. The patient grabbed his rifle and then sat down on the deck with the rifle resting on his legs. Other troopers who saw what had happened, stood back and asked him to settle down and to take things easy. The patient started to yell and scream unintelligibly and then levelled the rifle at the troopers, threateningly.

Ida was strolling on the deck and walked around the corner. She saw what was happening. She was behind the patient, and he had not seen her. She quietly took off her shoes and crept up to him and then put both of her arms around his neck and squeezed tightly.

He dropped the rifle and tried to force her arms apart. The watching troopers quickly came to her aid and soon overpowered the patient.

In the meantime, the unconscious trooper had come to and picked up his rifle. 'It only had one bullet in it, anyhow.'

Ida was shaken and needed the inevitable cup of strong tea. Unfortunately, the patient spent the rest of his voyage locked in the ship's brig.

Ida was questioned by an officer, who unbeknown to her, recommended that she be considered for a commendation.

The journey across the Indian Ocean seemed to last forever. They sailed past the Cocos Keeling Islands and gave the residents a few toots on the foghorn. Then came their first sight of Australia – the Western Australian sandy coastline.

The "Roaring Forties" winds were favourable and sailing through the Great Australian Bight was like a pleasure cruise. They sunbathed, read or just walked the decks, enjoying the kind weather. The call of – 'There's the Heads', brought the troops and medical team on deck.

They entered Port Phillip Bay on the incoming ride and then headed north to Port Melbourne. They could see vehicles driving along the bay roads, smoke rising from the chimneys, gum trees lining the roads. They were home again at long last.

Prior to disembarking, the colonel held a brief meeting with them, advising their next posting had been confirmed. A new military hospital had been established in a Melbourne northern suburb. They had been granted one month leave and were then to report to the hospital and, finally, the team was staying together. He wished them good luck and a happy leave with kith and kin.

Ida was transported to the Melbourne transport officer's office to receive her travel ticket and then waited two hours for the train to depart.

An elderly gentleman sat alongside and said, 'Aren't you too young to be going to the war.' She burst out crying. The man walked away, puzzled.

Her parents knew she would be home that week but not the day. They took turns greeting each train. Her father was the lucky one. He spotted her through the carriage window. Hugs and kisses were natural – nearly four years from home. When her mother saw her, she was overcome with emotion and had to sit down. They had a quiet evening together without discussing the war. There was plenty of local gossip to catch up on.

Over the next week she visited Jane and Andrew and had lunch with them twice. Jane asked about Jimmy and how he seemed.

She was still getting his letters, but Ida had met with him several times!

Suddenly Ida realised she was the first one home. Where were Jimmy and Terry?

Ida was walking to the hairdresser when a well-dressed young man stopped before her.

'You're a nurse, aren't you?'

Ida stopped and answered, cautiously, 'Yes, do I know you?'

He replied, 'Well, yes and no. You took me to hospital and helped repair my knee several years ago. I'm William Joyce and I'd like to give you a belated thank you. When I recovered, I was told you had returned to Melbourne.'

Ida nodded. 'I remember now. How is the knee?'

'Just so so. I couldn't join the army because of it. Can I buy you lunch as a thank you?'

'Not today. I have an appointment, but we could meet tomorrow at the hotel dining room. Say at noon?'

William nodded. 'Agreed. Goodbye until then.'

When Ida returned home, it took her several months to feel comfortable in the local community. The difference to the easy-going local surroundings, from her overseas military discipline, the noise, smells and the horrors of the war took time for a change of mental attitude.

William and Ida became good friends, which slowly became more so. He was tolerant with her, as he appreciated that she needed time to become her old self after four years of war experiences.

Twelve months after their first meeting, Ida and William married and settled on his parents' farm to manage his holdings. His parents then retired to a house by the sea.

CHAPTER SIX

The Desert

It was a long, hot and dusty ride in the Army truck to Cairo. The airfield was the same – hot, dry and dusty. Major Wilson was away for the day, but Jimmy was expected and shown to his quarters. The airfield was busy with flights taking off and landing each minute. Jimmy soon realised they were the same airplanes practising take-off and landings.

Next morning, Major Wilson met Jimmy in the mess for breakfast. He was a born leader. He was tall with a commanding presence, affable but positive in his speech. He greeted Jimmy and sat with him. He said he had received a communique from London advising him that Jimmy would be attached to his squadron, "to evaluate the performance of the squadron pilots and maintenance standards".

This was a surprise to Jimmy. He advised Major Wilson he had been told he would be given his orders on arrival there.

The major replied, 'I'm busy with meetings today. Meet me in my office at zero nine hundred hours tomorrow to sort this out.'

That afternoon a letter arrived addressed to Jimmy advising him of his orders which were identical to the orders the major had received plus an itemised list of specific queries required to be addressed.

The meeting next morning consisted of the major, three other officers and Jimmy. The air was one of anger and concern.

Major Wilson started. 'Can you tell us why you're here?'

Jimmy handed his orders and the attachments to him. 'That's all I know, sir.'

The office door opened just then and the major was handed a telegram. After reading it, he sat back. 'This explains why. Briefly, the powers that be have formed a new section to ensure certain standards are met. Lt Symons is on secondment from the Avro Company and has been tasked with that duty and to visit R.F.C. squadrons as directed.' He looked at Jimmy. 'What are your criteria?'

Jimmy answered, 'It's with the orders I gave you.'

The major flicked through them. 'Lieutenant, we need to talk. Excuse us, gentlemen, for ten minutes.' The three officers left.

The major said, 'I will support your survey of the squadron, but I would like your assurance that any discrepancies you find you will do me the courtesy of informing me before Headquarters.'

Jimmy replied, 'Yes, you have my word. This will not be a witch hunt. If you can fix it before I leave, nothing more will be said or reported.'

'Good. I appreciate your frankness.'

The other officers came back in and sat down. The major repeated what Jimmy had said and asked for questions.

One officer asked, 'Can we ask your qualifications for this survey?'

Jimmy answered, 'I am a pilot with forty-five flight hours, mainly as a ferry pilot in the UK and Europe. I have flown over German lines dropping pamphlets. Sometimes I returned with bullet holes from ground fire but managed to avoid German fighters. I am a qualified British aircraft mechanic and prior to my secondment worked for the Avro Company as a technical officer and ferry pilot.'

One pilot asked, 'Where have I seen you before?'

Jimmy said, 'I was in Alexandra last month.'

'Yes, you were involved in solving the rigging problem. I was there on the day you did the test flight. You did a good job finding the cause.'

As there were no more questions, the major dismissed the men.

It was arranged that Jimmy would be accompanied by a pilot for a week and the following week by a senior mechanic.

The squadron was operational and busy, mainly identifying the Turks' military movements and at times some bombing raids.

Jimmy watched the start and take-off procedures. Some pilots mainly relied on their ground crews to do the preflight inspections and fuel and oil checks, contrary to required procedures. Jimmy discretely recorded their names. One pilot did not take time to warm his engine and oil. Generally, the pilots were very professional.

The hangar was always busy, particularly with the rigging tension checks and repairs to the fuselage, wings and control surface skin and stone damage to the propellors. Several times he noticed the supervisors did not double check the mechanic who had initially checked the rigging tension, but other than that, the maintenance was as per the manual requirements. His report was positive, and it complimented the squadron's overall performance.

He met with the major and handed him his findings. He looked up and said, 'Thank you. I will ensure these problems are attended to promptly. When will you tell these men of your findings, and will I receive a copy of your report to London?'

Jimmy nodded. 'Yes, certainly you will receive a copy, but no, you will inform your staff of my findings and follow up the results. Not me.' The major was about to argue but changed his mind.

Jimmy forwarded a telegram to London, advising a report was on the way and requested his next orders. He waited five days to receive an answer. He was ordered to report to the 4th Australian Light Horse for a special assignment.

When Major Wilson found out about Jimmy's new assignment, he offered to have him flown to their base.

An aircraft had an engine failure only a mile or so from the Light Horse base. The pilot had walked into the base and gave a vague report. He said the engine cut out and he ditched the aircraft and as it was due for an overhaul it was not worth recovering. He then went to Cairo. A Light Horse company had found the aircraft and placed a guard on it, pending a decision on whether it was to be recovered.

The colonel met Jimmy as he stepped from the aircraft. Jimmy saluted the colonel.

'Good, you have finally arrived. Briefly, we have an abandoned aircraft near our base. I want to know if it can be repaired. You're temporarily transferred to our regiment. Can you ride?'

'Yes, I rode in rodeos before coming overseas.'

'Good. Captain Day will get you kitted out as a Light Horse officer and then show you to your quarters. Tomorrow be at the map room at zero nine hundred hours. You will leave to ride to the aircraft at ten hundred hours. That's all.' He walked away.

Captain Day smiled. 'Yes, he's a human dynamo and a very good leader. Let's get you your new uniform.'

The map showed the base, the railway track and where the aircraft had been abandoned. The ride was to get Jimmy's expert opinion, whether it was worth recovering it intact or to dismantle it for parts for the nearby Australian Flyng Corps.

The aircraft's undercarriage had collapsed, several rigging wires had detached, and the right wing appeared to be out of alignment with two broken struts. On the plus side, the two bladed propellor was undamaged as it was horizontal and had not struck the ground and damaged the engine internally. The fuselage and left wing appeared undamaged. He determined the aircraft could be repaired. It was an Avro 504K and Jimmy had the maintenance manuals with him. The problem was how to transport the aircraft to the base.

When he debriefed the colonel, he asked, 'If I can get a flat railway carriage, could we lift it onto it?'

Jimmy answered, 'Yes, I can remove the engine. It would take a team of ten or so men to lift it.'

The colonel, 'Do it, starting tomorrow.'

Jimmy went to the vehicle maintenance store and collected the necessary tools.

The next day they rode out from their base in the morning with the colonel leading. The team had the engine removed by noon. The team then slowly lifted the aircraft and then set it down again. The plan would work.

The following day at noon, a small locomotive arrived with a flat top carriage attached. The aircraft was loaded with difficulty, followed by loading the damaged undercarriage and engine. All were tied down onto the flat top and away it went towards the base with several horsemen on board. The others rode back to base with their horses.

The return was not without incident. A lone tree was overhanging the train line and would hit the wing. A sergeant went forward, dug a small hole at the base of the tree, stepped back and lobbed a hand grenade into the hole. He ran back to a small mound and lay flat behind it. The explosion shattered the tree. Branches were removed from the train line and the train continued its journey.

These troopers don't mess around, Jimmy thought.

The colonel had a large canvas tent erected to shelter the aircraft and the workers from the elements. The first job was to repair and fit the undercarriage. Each Light Horse brigade had a blacksmith-farrier trooper. The bent struts holding the wheels were straightened by the brigade's blacksmith and refitted to the fuselage within two days.

Jimmy fitted the two replacement struts he had flown from Cairo. He then commenced rigging the straining wires and checked their tension. He then installed the engine. He gave the wooden propellor a lamination-delamination test by tapping opposite sections of the propellor with a coin and listening attentively. Both tap sounds needed to be the same, which they were, meaning the propellor wooden sections had not separated from each other and it was serviceable for further use.

Each day the colonel would visit the makeshift hangar and ask for a progress report on when he could expect the aircraft to be ready to fly.

Jimmy replied, 'I need at least another week, a maximum of ten days.'

The colonel sat down and said quietly, 'Confidentially, in three weeks we will be embarking on a major push against the Turks in the Sinai, and I hope to use this aircraft as a Light Horse observer aircraft. I think your test flights will coincide with my observation requirements.' He paused and whispered, *'If you take my drift.'* Raising his voice to normal again, 'Would you be happy doing these flights?'

Jimmy answered, 'I do as I'm ordered and as I'm attached to the Light Horse, I don't see a problem, sir.'

The colonel stood up. 'Good. Keep what I told you to yourself. I'll let the brigadier know. I have nothing against the R.F.C. or the A.F.C. but this will allow us to respond instantly to the Turks' movements without having any communication delay.'

Jimmy replied, 'Yes, I understand your reasoning, sir. However, your so-called "airfield" needs the rocks removed. There is a risk of propellor damage and ruptured tyres.'

The colonel nodded. 'Leave that to me.'

Jimmy had the assistance of three former motor mechanics to help him with the wire rigging. Several brackets attaching the rigging to the undercarriage had snapped. He obtained the parts with the struts from the Avro parts store in Cairo. Replacing the brackets was easy but the rigging was time consuming. Slowly they progressed. He checked both wing angles with a clinometer and was delighted to see both were set to the correct angle. He had two mechanics repeat his tension checks and they agreed with the manual.

His final inspection required cutting small holes in the right wing. He checked three crucial areas of the internal spar joints and was satisfied they were sound. On the ninth day, they wheeled the aircraft out of the makeshift hangar for an engine test. The fuel and oil were drained and refilled after their filters had been replaced. The spark plugs were also changed after the cylinders had been compression tested and found to be within limits.

After three attempts the engine started. Jimmy allowed it to run at idle for ten minutes, then shut the engine down. After the engine cooled, he pulled the fuel and oil filters to check they were clean. A quick inspection of the control cables, rudder and fuselage was carried out to his satisfaction. He then decided he would taxi, and test fly the aircraft the next day.

The colonel was there to see the test flight. After starting up and warming the engine, he opened the throttle. The engine ran to perfection. He taxied out to the airfield and headed the aircraft into the wind.

The colonel, true to his word, had ordered the runway cleared of rocks. He opened the throttle and increased speed as he slowly lifted clear of the airfield. He then set the aircraft down. He taxied back and increased power and this time he took off. He climbed to five hundred feet and did two circuits of the base before landing.

The colonel took Jimmy aside when he was back on the ground. 'Can you find an excuse to keep the aircraft here?'

'Yes, it's due for an overhaul and I can do it here. I'm authorised to certify an aircraft overhaul.'

'Good, we need a high altitude flight along the Sinai coast to Gaza and fly back five miles inland. We have information the Turks are moving. I want facts. I don't want you to be seen by the Turks. Fly high and use cloud cover as necessary. How long would it be before you can be ready to fly?'

Jimmy answered, 'Maximum one hour and I will need an observer.'

'Alright, take off at dawn tomorrow,' he was ordered.

The colonel assigned Lieutenant George Curly, an officer with navigation experience, to be his observer. The flight started at first light. There was scattered cloud down to three thousand feet and light winds. The coast appeared as a blue sea meeting sandy beaches and some small villages. A peaceful sight.

They climbed to an altitude of four thousand feet and commenced looking at the foreshore. Gaza appeared ahead, and about a mile before reaching there, they saw a large encampment of a Turkish military force.

George made a sign to turn inland. Jimmy flew inland for five minutes then turned and headed back to base.

When they landed, there was a vehicle waiting to take them to the brigadier's office. The office had a large map on the wall of the coastline.

The colonel asked Lt Curly to relate the survey flight's findings.

George had written notes during the flight and read from them. In summary, he said, 'A large Turkish army, estimated at least five thousand men are assembled on the coast but no troops were sighted inland, not even scouting parties.'

The brigadier stood up and said, 'Well done and I want you to fly the same route again in two days.'

The flight was repeated as ordered with the same report. No movement had occurred. On the third flight, they found that the Turks had spread their troops in a line along the beach and back inland for about two thousand yards.

The brigadier was delighted. 'The Turks expect us to come via the coast.' This information was relayed to the general immediately.

Jimmy was asked to deliver an urgent despatch to Cairo and return with some mail. He and a mechanic had delivered the despatch and were descending when they saw an aircraft on the ground and a pilot waving to them.

He flew low over him and began looking for somewhere to land. A road was three hundred yards to his right. The mechanic wrote a note telling the downed pilot to walk to the road. He put the note in a cleaning cloth, tied it to a spanner and dropped it to him.

When he read it, the pilot waved and immediately headed towards the road.

As Jimmy turned to line up and land, a group of Bedouins appeared from behind a hill riding in the direction of the aircraft. These Arab tribes were unpredictable.

Jimmy decided to scatter them. He flew low behind them. The horses began rearing as they heard the aircraft approaching and the engine roaring ahead. Most riders were thrown. Jimmy continued his landing and when the pilot reached the aircraft, he told him the airfield was only five minutes flying away. He told him to lay flat on the wing next to the fuselage and to hold on to the wire brackets and not to move.

The Arabs began shooting at them. Bullets were whizzing over their heads. Jimmy opened throttle and they were soon airborne. As he turned towards base, he felt a searing pain in his right calf muscle.

They landed successfully and taxied to the hangar.

The colonel angrily asked, 'Where the hell have you been? You were expected an hour ago.'

'Well, sir, we rescued a downed pilot', Jimmy answered.

The colonel replied, 'Are you mad? There are only two of you. What are you talking about?'

The rescued pilot stepped forward and said, 'No, he's not mad, he rescued me.' He explained the rescue to the colonel.

The colonel shook his head. 'Unbelievable!' and walked away.

Jimmy and the mechanic climbed from the aircraft, both bloodied. Jimmy promptly fell over. An ambulance arrived and took them to the airfield First Aid Post. The mechanic had a bullet wound to his hip and Jimmy, a bullet that passed through his right calf muscle. Each of them had been hit by a bullet when Jimmy turned the aircraft to fly back to base.

In hospital they were treated as heroes. They were embarrassed at first, but then they just accepted the accolades. Why not!

The mechanic's bullet passed through the fleshy part just above his hip, but there was no internal damage. To use the doctor's phrase, he was soon "patched up" with a few stiches.

Jimmy had a small bullet enter on the outer side of his right calf muscle and, when exiting, had made a much larger hole.

The senior doctor had seen war injuries before and was unfazed. After cleaning the area, the wound on Jimmy's outer calf were stitched together. The exit hole was another matter. It was much larger. The hole was plugged to stop the bleeding and the calf bandaged tightly and it remained so for two days. When next inspected the bleeding had stopped, and the wound was then stitched. The dressing was replaced, and the calf rebound daily for the next seven days. By this time Jimmy was up and about and walking with a walking stick. The doctor said he could fly when he felt the calf wound would not be a problem.

The aircraft had twelve bullet holes in the fuselage and the wings. Jimmy's mechanics came to see him in hospital to show him a diagram of the aircraft and the location of the holes. They had enlarged the bullet holes so they could inspect the inner frames and ribs. The majority had caused no damage. The only frame damaged was in the fuselage alongside the pilot's seat. This could have been the bullet that struck his calf. The frame was accessible, but they left it for Jimmy to decide on the repair scheme.

The colonel walked in and asked, 'How are you progressing? I need you up and about.'

'Good luck, sir. I'm discharged as of now. I'm going to the hangar to carry out a repair I need to do.'

The colonel nodded. 'Come and see me tomorrow.'

Jimmy visited the hangar and looked over the aircraft. The mechanics had done a good repair job.

The cockpit frame required special attention. He heated some glue and then pressed the damaged frame outwards to open the crack. He then slowly dripped the liquid glue into the crack. After applying a liberal quantity into it, he pushed the damaged section together. Finally. he wrapped the cracked area with thin wire along the whole of the length of the damage.

The story about the rescue soon spread. When he visited the colonel, he said, 'The general asked me about your escapade and was impressed. He has recommended you for a Military Cross and your mechanic for a Military Medal.

'Now to get back to business. Tomorrow, I want you and Curly to fly up the coast again and see if anything has changed. We start our movement in two days, and we need to know if the Turks have changed their deployment. This time, on your return flight, I want you to fly further inland and see what's out there. I want you to do one flight at first light and another in the late afternoon. Any questions?'

Jimmy answered, 'No. I just hope the weather is favourable with a few clouds to help provide us with some cover.'

The weather for their early flight was calm with clear skies. Jimmy had got into the habit of singing when he reached cruise altitude. Today he flew lower, at three thousand feet.

The two of them were able to talk to each other through a voice tube. Jimmy sang reasonably well, and they ended up singing together. Canon fire abruptly interrupted their duet. They had been spotted. Jimmy climbed to five thousand feet out of reach of the shells.

The Turkish Army was still in the same position as the previous week. Nothing had changed. They turned inland. They spotted several squads of Turks on camels. He guessed they were scouts. They then flew back to base.

After they handed in their report, they had lunch and a short nap.

As ordered, they took off again along the coast in the afternoon. They spotted some activity inland and descended to have a closer look. At fifteen hundred feet they could see wheel tracks leading to a river. On the river were several dhows with Turkish troops on board. They were spotted and received a volley of rifle fire. Suddenly the aircraft started vibrating violently. The propellor had been splintered. Jimmy closed the throttle and turned the fuel supply off. He looked for somewhere to crash land.

In the distance was an oasis with a Bedouin camp and road half a mile from their camp. He aimed the stricken aircraft towards the road. They were losing altitude rapidly, but they managed to reach the road and landed heavily. The undercarriage collapsed and two lower wings broke away from their attachments.

Jimmy and George climbed from the wrecked aircraft and considered their options. Really there was only one – walk to the oasis and hope the tribe was friendly. Each of them had a revolver but they would be of little benefit against an unfriendly tribe.

When they reached the top of a sand dune, they saw six Arabs riding towards them on camels.

The meeting was not friendly. They immediately took their revolvers from them and then tied their hands behind them. None of them knew English. They were made to walk behind the camels and arrived at the oasis exhausted and very thirsty. They were taken to a large tent and gestured to kneel.

In walked an unsmiling Arab dressed in a white robe with gold braiding. He was obviously the tribe's leader. 'Why are you here?' he asked in good English.

Jimmy answered, 'We were flying back to our base and didn't know you were here.'

The Arab looked at him. 'Where is your base?'

'In Cairo,' Jimmy answered.

The Arab said to another, 'Lock them up for now. We will talk with them tomorrow when they are hungry.'

They were taken to small tent and told to sit down. George was a little slow and was savagely hit with a rifle butt to his face.

The next morning two Arabs came to take them back to the main tent. One of them saw Jimmy's ring and attempted to take it off. When it couldn't be removed, he drew his dagger and severed his finger. Jimmy collapsed in shock and had to be carried into the tent. An Arab bandaged his hand and gave him some water.

The Arab leader asked to see the ring and was surprised to see it had the local Sheik's emblem on it.

He asked Jimmy, 'Where did you get this ring?'

He replied, 'It was a present from Khalifa, the Sheik's son.'

'Liar, you stole it', said the Arab. 'He will be here in three days, and we will ask him and then we will kill you.'

The sound of musical instruments advised the arrival of the Sheik's son, Khalifa Bin Ali Arn. When he was handed something it caused him to sit upright in anger. It was the ring.

He said, 'Bring him to me now. Who is responsible for this?' The Arab who cut off Jimmy's finger stepped forward, expecting praise, but it was not to be.

Jimmy and George were taken into the main tent.

Seated on a large chair was Khalifa. He had his head down and was listening to the local Arab leader.

Jimmy walked into the tent and looked at Khalifa, who stood up with the bearing of authority.

Khalifa walked to Jimmy and hugged him, to the surprise of all. Asking, 'What have they done to you?' Jimmy didn't answer.

But George did, pointing to the Arab who severed Jimmy's finger. 'That bastard did it.'

Khalifa asked the Arab leader, 'Is that true?' The Arab leader nodded, 'He has shamed us.' Khalifa said something in Arabic. Two Arabs took the offender out of the tent. He was screaming. Then there was silence.

Jimmy and George were then treated to an excellent meal. They chatted for several hours.

Jimmy asked, 'Can you get us back to our base? They'll be wondering where we are.'

'Yes, you will be delivered safe to your base. But please re-accept my ring. It has good memories, as well as bad ones.'

Jimmy nodded.

The next morning, after bidding farewell, Jimmy and George were escorted to the base by six of Khalifa's personal guards.

When they reported to the colonel, he asked, 'Where the hell have you two been? You had me worried.'

After telling the story, the colonel shook his head. 'You never cease to amaze me. Write a report and I'll let the general know you two have returned and what to do with you, Symons.'

They were both given a week off from duties. Jimmy wondered what his future posting would be. He would like to be transferred to the Australian Light Horse but didn't know whether he should ask or not.

A week later, the decision was made for him. The RAF advised that Lt Symons could return to the Avro Co. as a Reserve Officer. There would be no more assignments for him.

The colonel sent for Jimmy and together they visited the general's office.

The general waved them to be seated. 'I see that the RAF have dispensed with your service. What are your thoughts for the future?'

Jimmy took a deep breath and replied, 'As an Australian, I would like to transfer to the Australian Light Horse. I have enjoyed my time here and feel I'm already an honorary Light Horseman. I believe my aviation skills would be an asset and, if not, I can ride as a Horseman.'

The general looked at the colonel. 'What do you think, colonel?'

He nodded. 'Sir, I agree with Symons' request to be transferred to us.'

The general stood up signifying the end of the meeting. 'Put it writing to me and we will see what I can do.'

As they left the colonel said, 'The general normally gets what wants. Be patient.'

Two weeks later, Jimmy received a letter addressed to Captain J Symons. It was a letter advising him that he had been transferred to the Australian Light Horse Brigade and additionally promoted to a permanent rank of captain. He was to report to the same colonel.

The colonel ordered Jimmy to work with George Curly on the maps they had previously surveyed and identify what oasis and waterholes they had found to determine a route for the brigade to follow to their ultimate destination – Jerusalem. They needed to consider which areas had large dunes that needed to be avoided. When the route was drawn on a new map, the colonel sent out a scout team, mainly to see if the main sand dunes had not moved due to the strong winds. The scouts came back and agreed with the new map.

The general was delighted with the new map and decided his strategy on the information.

Jimmy and George were permitted to accompany the regiments as combatants.

Jimmy was thrilled to see the long row of Horsemen in front of them disappearing into the distance. Although they had to stay with the colonel and view the skirmish from a nearby hill, they could still see the hand to hand fighting and the Horsemen dismounting and firing their rifles. The Turks retreated time and time again. They started surrendering and the remainder disbanded. The colonel said to nobody in particular, 'I think we will be in Jerusalem soon.'

The prisoners were a problem. There were so many. Jimmy and George ended up guarding over three hundred Turks by themselves.

A captain and several Horsemen rode up and told Jimmy they were looking for a Turkish general, missing two fingers from his right hand.

His team started to check the prisoners. Jimmy noticed a group of ten prisoners huddled in a corner. He pointed them out to the captain.

The captain said, 'Ride up the back of them. I'll split them from the main group. Be alert; he could be armed.'

Jimmy drew his revolver and trotted up behind the group. As the captain began to separate them from the main group of prisoners, one Turk stood up and ran at Jimmy. The Arab had a curved knife raised and he was shouting, 'Allah AK—". He didn't finish. Jimmy fired his revolver twice. The two bullets hit the Turk in the chest, and he immediately fell down – dead.

The captain jumped from his horse and looked at the Turk's right hand. It had two fingers missing.

The captain said, 'Well done. We got him. He was a dangerous general. We have cut off the head of the snake.'

Jimmy was a bit shaken after shooting the Turkish general.

But his colonel said, 'That's war; move on.' The colonel then assigned Jimmy to courier duties. He was to return to the UK with a security satchel accompanied by George Curly. They were to travel by warship non-stop.

While in the UK he was to be presented with his Military Cross. On arrival they went to Whitehall and handed over the security documents. After two days sightseeing they then went to the investiture for Jimmy to receive his M.C. Three days later they were sailing back to Egypt.

Jimmy started to have nightmares and headaches. The doctor checked his vital signs and said, 'Young fellow, you're going home. Your nerves are shattered; you've been here too long.'

Within a week Jimmy was heading home on a packed troopship. He had said goodbye to the friends he had made. He would miss George and the colonel. But was looking forward to going home. Before he left Egypt he wrote to Mr Sharpe and told him of events and that he was returning to Australia.

The voyage home was enjoyable. The seas were mostly calm and the days sunny with little wind. Some of the troops were musicians and most evenings after dinner they assembled at the bow and played well-known songs. The troops would sing regardless of the quality of their voices.

To hear hundreds of trooper voices singing together signified the ultimate in comradeship. This was indicative of the character of the Australian Military Service personnel.

CHAPTER SEVEN

Home Again

Jimmy's first sight of Australia was the Western Australian coast. The sandy brown cliffs brought tears to his eyes. He had been away for nearly four years.

He sat quietly on a bollard and began to think about what the future held for him. Jane's letters had been a source of comfort, but he wondered if it would be the same when they met again. Her latest photograph showed the happy smiling girl he had kept in his memory.

He was unsure what he would do for a living now. His father and brother had successfully managed to develop and prosper the property in his absence. They didn't need him. The aircraft business in Australia was in its infancy but he wasn't sure if he could fit in. There was, perhaps, the Avro offer. Or maybe he could work on his parents' farm or help out at Jane's parents' farm. But really his first objective was to get married and worry about employment matters later.

The families, and Jane in particular, knew he was heading home but had no idea of his arrival date. He had not been able to advise them, as he hadn't known. He decided to telephone them both from Melbourne.

The trip through the Bight was relatively calm compared to the last time when he sailed to England, four years ago, into a viscous storm. He still remembered the waves they had encountered sailing into the "Roaring Forties". Now the sun was shining and some of the crewmen were fishing from the stern. One sailor caught a small shark and donated it to the chief cook. Most diners that evening sampled the tasty fish.

The Victorian coastline was visible when he went up on deck for his daily walkaround. It was hazy in the morning sun but as the day warmed, Jimmy could see the Victorian shoreline and buildings in the distance.

Eventually they lined up their course and entered through the Port Phillip Bay heads and, after another change of course, the ship headed up the bay towards Port Melbourne. They arrived early morning as Melbournians were waking to head to work. Smoke was rising from the shoreline houses. He was back in Australia in time for Christmas 1918.

The deck rails were lined with returning servicemen and nurses, eagerly looking forward to their homecoming. Some were carrying injuries, but their faces were aglow with happiness to have returned.

The deck was covered with personal effects and souvenirs. Hopefully customs would not be too officious. It took a few hours for the ship to be moored alongside a pier. The tugboats had been very busy as they patiently **waited** for their turn to be assisted to the pier. The pier was crowded with people who were waving, waiting to greet the returning diggers.

When the gangways were connected to the ship, the first people to come aboard were the dreaded customs officers, who, surprising, only did a few token searches. Some wore Boer War ribbons. This was probably the reason for their leniency. After they left, there was a mad scramble to get ashore.

Jimmy was in no hurry. He watched as some found their welcoming family and friends. Some returning servicemen were left standing alone. Wondering why, Jimmy felt for them. Perhaps a wife or girlfriend who no longer cared or worse, leaving them returning from war and returning to – nothing!

It reminded Jimmy of an incident that had happened in France. As a newly commissioned Reserve Lieutenant, he had been sent to resolve some mechanical faults on Avro aircraft. They were Avro 504K's used for observing German troop movements. During his time in France, he shared a tent with an infantry officer. William Joyce was a seasoned veteran who had served in the Boer War in 1900 as a boy soldier. Jimmy found him an affable and likeable person. Regardless of their age difference they were comparable tent mates.

William's demeanour changed dramatically one day after receiving a letter from home; he didn't want to talk about it. Two days later he led a platoon into battle and was killed. A corporal came to collect his personal effects.

Jimmy asked, 'Can you tell me what happened?'

He replied, 'Well we had captured the trench and were rounding up the prisoners, when he picked up a Lewis gun and attacked the next trench by himself. Why he did it, we just don't know. He killed most of the Germans before he was killed.' When the corporal lifted the bed, some papers fell onto the floor and Jimmy picked them up and saw they were addressed to William. He advised the corporal that, as they were personal, he would give them to the colonel.

Jimmy was shuffling the papers into a neat group, when he couldn't help noticing the words – *I'm sorry but that's the way it is. Our marriage is over. Goodbye, Will – Jill and Oscar.* He knew they had been married for over ten years and had a boy named Oscar.

Jimmy was in a quandary. He decided to send all of William's letters back to his wife with a short covering note from him. One year later, Jimmy was invited to an Awards Investiture Day in London.

He was there to receive a Military Cross for his desert rescue. But lo and behold William's wife was there to receive a Military Cross – awarded to Lt Willliam Joyce – posthumously. Jimmy was furious and waited until the majority of people had dispersed.

He approached Jill. 'Mrs Joyce, I would like to introduce myself.'

She looked at him. 'I don't think I know you.'

'I'm Lt Jimmy Symons and I was your husband's tent mate at the time he was killed.'

She went white and sat in a chair. She now recognised the name "Symons" from the covering letter she had received with the letters she had written to William, including the fateful last one.

Jimmy ruthlessly continued, 'He died because of the last letter you wrote to him. He lost the will to live without his son. You have no right to have his medal. It should be given to his son, Oscar. Is he here?'

During Jimmy's outburst, a man had been standing alongside her, quietly listening. He interrupted Jimmy. 'Yes, he's here and, Captain Symons, I agree. Jill, call Oscar over here and pin the medal on him. It would be wrong for you to keep it knowing what happened.'

A smartly dressed young boy approached them. Jill said, 'Oscar here is your father's medal for you to keep and cherish.' She kissed him.

Jimmy nodded to them, saluted young Oscar and then walked away.

Jimmy collected his goods and chattels, hailed a coach and went to the country line station. The next train was leaving in three hours. He went to the Military Rail Transport Office to collect a ticket and to telephone home. He was allowed a minute per call. He rang home first as he knew he would spend more time talking with Jane.

'Hello, Mum. I'm in Melbourne.' Silence, then he could hear his mother crying and calling his father.

After a pause, his father was on the phone. 'Welcome home, son. Where are you now?'

'I'm in Melbourne and I'm coming by train. I should arrive at around eleven o'clock tonight. We can talk more then. I'm going to telephone Jane now. Bye for now and make Mum a cup of tea.'

'Bye, son. It's good to hear your voice.'

Jane answered the telephone. 'Hello, Jane Hay speaking.'

Jimmy answered, 'And this is Jimmy Symons speaking from Melbourne. I'm back in Melbourne and I'll arrive at the station around eleven o'clock tonight. It will be good to see you again.'

Jane was still catching her breath after hearing the good news.

'Jane, it's so good to hear your voice again. I've really missed you.'

She then started to cry.

The transport officer waved to Jimmy. 'You've had your time, sir.'

Jimmy nodded to him and said to Jane, 'I have to finish the call. I'll see you soon. Bye, my love.'

It was a long and lonely wait at the cold dark station, but at least he was able to get a sandwich, a hot cup of tea and yesterday's newspaper. The train arrived on time with only a few carriages. After depositing his chest and suitcase in the baggage car, he boarded the train and soon found a seat in an empty compartment and fell asleep.

He was in uniform, complete with the emu feather, except for his revolver. At the last stop he was joined by a local resident who knew him from their school days. A conversation soon started.

His school colleague had been in a class above Jimmy. He said, 'I arrived back from France last month. I'm glad I won't be going back. I have a bullet in my shoulder. What about you? Did you come out unmarked.'

Jimmy thought for a second or two before answering. 'Physically, I have a bullet through my calf and a severed finger. Mentally, I still have unsettling dreams. But, yes, I survived, as did you.' Just then an elderly woman entered the compartment and the two men immediately stopped talking about the war.

The woman asked, 'Are you a Light Horseman? My nephew is one of them, in the desert.'

Jimmy answered, 'Yes, I am, madam.'

She replied, 'It must be an exciting life, being able to see all the pyramids and holy cities.'

'Yes, it certainly is.' The two soldiers looked at each other and said nothing more, thinking how little the people in Australia realised the carnage occurring on the battle fields in Europe and the desert. The woman had started knitting and was quietly humming a tune, oblivious to the world.

The train slowly came to a halt. Jimmy was delighted to see it had stopped right opposite where his family and Jane were waiting. His mother reached him first, hugged him and kissed him, tears in her eyes. His father and brother shook his hands.

Jane was standing back a little from the group. When his mother let him go, he went to Jane and kissed her. They hugged each other, not saying a word. Jane was crying; Jimmy was close to crying as well.

Greetings were temporarily forgotten as the station master reminded passengers to collect their luggage from the baggage car. His father and brother went with him. Jane stayed with his mother.

His father had a two-horse coach as transport to home. Jimmy and Jane sat quietly in the back seat with Jimmy's arm around her shoulders.

Jimmy's mother had a supper laid out to celebrate his homecoming. His father offered him a cold beer and they toasted his return.

A speech was required. 'Firstly, thank you for your letters over the years. In the quietness of a desert night, at times I felt I was still here. I know I have been away a long time, but I have now achieved my dream of a career in aviation and, most of all, I survived the war. However, at the back of my mind always, was Jane. She was my strength and guiding light over the years. You are a treasure. When times were tough, I would think of you to help keep my sanity and my determination alive. You are a most remarkable woman who has waited for me long enough. Now we have some planning to do. Thank you.' Applause! and he bowed to his captive audience. An hour later, the evening was over, leaving Jimmy and Jane by themselves.

They walked arm in arm up the dark lane, enjoying each other's company.

Jimmy said, 'Tomorrow you and I should pack a picnic hamper and have some time with each other.' He kissed her goodnight. It was late, so Jane stayed overnight and slept in Michael's bedroom.

Jimmy was awake first and went to Jane's room and knocked on the bedroom door. 'Time to get up, Jane.'

Jane answered, 'Come in. I'm awake.' She was still in bed and was wearing Michael's oversized pyjamas. He bent over the bed to kiss her. She sat up to meet him when her top opened revealing her breasts.

Jimmy kissed her and then fondled her breast. Jane said nothing, she just returned his kiss and put her arms around his neck.

Jimmy then tried to get Jane to lay back on the bed.

Jane immediately sat up. 'We've waited this long; we can wait another few weeks.'

Begrudgingly Jimmy nodded.

He then borrowed a dressing gown from his father and returned to Jane's bedroom. She was now sitting on the bed in her underwear, smiling and looking pretty as a picture, waiting for him. They both attended breakfast in their dressing gowns.

After harnessing the horse, he loaded the hamper. They drove quietly, viewing the scene around them.

Jimmy suddenly said, 'I think we need to have a long conversation. I would like to get married tomorrow but I have been away for so long a time. We need to be happy and comfortable with each other still.'

Jane sat quietly and didn't answer immediately. She was somewhat shocked by his unexpected words.

Jimmy sensed her feeling. 'I'm still in love with you and always will be, but I've been away from you for so long. I want to be fair to you and your feelings for me.'

Jane turned to him and replied angrily, 'Don't you ever frighten me again by talking like that. Of course, I love you. More so since you have been back these last few hours.' Leaning over, she kissed him firmly on the lips.

They stopped by a river bank, put the horse's nose bag on and sat on the grass embankment. Bird life was plentiful, and some ducks were swimming nearby. Europe and the war were far away.

Jane asked, 'What was the war like? It's hard to believe what we read in the paper.'

Jimmy had no intention of telling her the whole truth; he would only gloss over the realities. 'War for me was an eye opener to what evils man can do to each other. Yes, people die and get wounded. I was lucky only having a bullet through my calf muscle and losing a finger. I've seen heroic sights and I've seen cowardly acts. But who am I to judge? The stench from the mud and cold nights had to be experienced to be believed. The smell of gunpowder and sounds of guns firing stayed with me for days after I left France. The desert was different. It was hot and dry. Flying was difficult with the unpredictable sandstorms and winds. In the end I developed an attitude and blocked out the carnage. I've had enough of war.' He paused. 'However, I'm proud I did my service for Australia. Now no more of war. Time for a beer.'

Jane opened a bottle of ale and joined him in a drink. 'To the future.' She looked at Jimmy and took his hands in hers. 'Yes, I agree. What have you decided?'

Jimmy shrugged his shoulders. 'I know farming and aircraft. You tell me. I spent nearly four years, starting as a mechanic, then a technical officer and finally becoming a pilot, but I'm unsure what opportunities there are in Australia. I have several letters of introduction to some

Melbourne aircraft manufacturers. I would prefer to get married first and then consider what I should do.'

Jane nodded. 'Yes, I agree. Let's talk with our parents at a combined family dinner and start some planning.'

When they returned to their homes, they each told their parents of the need to start their wedding plans.

The dinner was planned to be held at Jimmy's parents' farm. Each parent had written a list of their thoughts and wishes for their wedding day. At the dinner, the first thing decided was the date of the wedding – four weeks from next Saturday. Then the parents took control, particularly the two mothers. One agreed to organise the reception and the catering, the other the church service and transport for the bridal party. The men volunteered to send out the invitations and oversee the timings and details on the day. The guest list would be decided by all of them at the table. Jane and Jimmy had little input. Jane's main concern was her wedding dress.

Jane and her mother would head to Melbourne and go shopping.

Jimmy intended to wear his uniform. He knew several members of the district Light Horse and wondered if they would provide a Guard of Honour when the bridal couple departed the church. It was not unusual in a country town.

The following Saturday, Jimmy and his father went shopping. The day was hot and sunny. They went to the local pub for a beer or two. They were well known in the district and several other drinkers gave them a friendly hello wave.

One of them was a member of the district Light Horse. He came over to them. 'I've been hoping to run into you. The major is hoping you might join our Light Horse troop.'

After shaking hands, Jimmy answered, 'I haven't even thought of it. But, yes, I probably will. I'm getting married in a few weeks. We can talk then. That reminds me, I was going to see the major and ask him if your troop would consider performing a Guard of Honour at our wedding.'

His friend laughed and nodded. 'Believe it or not, last week we were rehearsing that very drill. I'll ask the major to give you a call during the week. We'll talk more. Goodbye for now.'

Jimmy's father said, 'That was a stroke of luck. A military guard will look great. Let's keep it to ourselves as a surprise for the women.'

The wedding plans were coming together. Jane and her mother spent two days in Melbourne and returned looking satisfied. They told Jimmy nothing. Andrew Button was to be Jimmy's best man and Ida Whitty would be Jane's bridesmaid. The guest list was finalised at ninety five relatives and friends. Jane and Jimmy decided to live at Jimmy's parents' farm after they married. Thomas had selected Michael's room for them.

The view from the veranda was looking east down towards the dam and the main paddock across to the distant hill and its forest of gum trees. The morning sun made the veranda an excellent breakfast position. He had the room painted and installed new carpets and curtains. He also added some extra furniture. The room was nearly twice the size of Jimmy's current bedroom. Thomas wrote to Michael to tell him what he had done. He knew Michael would not object. Thomas had the smaller room repainted and replaced the carpets. Michael's odds and ends were then transferred to this room.

Two weeks before the wedding, Jimmy received a letter from Mr Sparks, who was still the works manager of the company. After the normal pleasantries, Mr Sparks asked,

> *Jimmy, please advise your interest in being a member of a works sales team to tour Australia in a few months.*
>
> *Two Avro 504 aircraft will arrive within two months at Melbourne. I would be obliged if you could oversee their assembly and certify them ready for flight. Your maintenance engineer's licence is valid, as you know, and the test pilot is an authorised examiner and instructor and could validate your pilot's licence, if you wish. Could you please answer by telegram soonest.*
> *Alan Sparks*
> *Works Manager*

Jimmy rode over to Jane's. She was sitting at the kitchen table and was surprised to see him before noon. He normally came over for dinner. He handed Jane the letter. 'I received it from England this morning. You need to read it before I answer.'

She read the letter twice, trying to appreciate its implications for them. Placing the letter on the table, she stood up and went to put the kettle on.

Jimmy sat quietly, waiting patiently.

Jane came back with two cups of tea. She wisely said, 'You are more affected than me. I will support whatever you decide. It's the career you wanted. I think you need to know more of this offer, such as the places you would visit, how long the project would last and would it lead to a full time position in Australia. Ask those questions and we can talk again when we know more.'

Jimmy nodded. 'Yes. Good thinking. I agree. I'll send a telegram off tomorrow and wait for his answers before we talk about it again.'

The following Saturday night, Jimmy and Jane attended a welcome home evening for the local returned military personnel.

Jimmy wore his uniform, complete with medals and emu feather. Ida attended in her uniform and medals. Terry was still overseas.

There were several other men and another – one woman in uniform – all looking very smart and proud. After dinner, the mayor gave a sterling speech. He was wearing his Boer war medals and spoke with the authority of one who had served. He presented each of the veterans with a council medal, suitably engraved.

When Jimmy went forward, the mayor asked him to say a few words.

Caught unawares, he paused and then he remembered what he had said at his family welcome home. He repeated the same words, emphasising the value of the letters they received from kith and kin.

After the speech, he went to the bar for a beer. A well-dressed man accompanied by the mayor approached him and was introduced. The man was a very wealthy and well-known local farmer. Jimmy had heard of Mr Cedric Coles, but this was the first time he had seen him, let alone met him.

Mr Coles asked Jimmy if he might meet with him during the week. He advised he had a proposition that might interest him. He said it involved aviation but said no more. They set a date and time and then went their separate ways. Jimmy was intrigued. Why would a wealthy farmer be interested in aviation?

The evening had a few more speeches and finished with the well-known barn dance, in which even the youngsters joined in.

He mentioned the invitation he had to visit Mr Coles to Jane. She had heard of him and seen him at some agriculture shows, but she knew nothing more than he was a wealthy local farmer.

They both visited Mr Cole's property. It was a pleasant day for a drive with the sun shining, no wind, only wildlife and farm animals in sight. The farm was extensive as far as the eye could see. The homestead was surrounded by three large barns and small holding paddocks. One looked new.

Mr Coles saw their gig coming up his driveway and walked to meet them. With a friendly wave and a 'Hello and welcome', he led their horse to a hitching pole and helped Jane alight. He shook Jimmy's hand and invited them into the homestead to an office and led them to a round table.

A maid had followed them in and asked, 'Would you care for tea and scones?'

Mr Coles answered for them. 'Yes. They have had a hot drive. Thank you, Mary.' After Mary had left he turned to Jimmy.

'Jimmy, no doubt you are curious as to why I have invited you here today.'

Jimmy nodded but said nothing.

'I am a widower. My wife, Marion, and I only had one son who was killed towards the end of the war in an aircraft crash in the desert. I believe you served in the desert as a pilot?'

Jimmy thought for a minute before answering. 'I spent nearly a year in the area. Did your son have a nick name?'

'Yes, he was called "Frosty",' Mr Coles answered.

Jimmy replied, 'Yes, I knew of him as "Frosty". I didn't know him personally, but I knew him by sight in the mess. He was in a different section to me. He was regarded as a good pilot. He was awarded the A.F.C., if my memory serves me correctly.' Speaking like this brought back some unpleasant memories for Jimmy.

Mr Coles was speechless for a while after hearing this revelation.

Opportunely, Mary returned with the tea and scones. This allowed calm to be restored around the table. Jane sat quietly listening to them talk.

After Mary had poured tea and left, Mr Coles said, 'I'm pleased I went to the Saturday evening function and met you.' He paused. 'I made the correct decision to invite you today. Prior to my son's death, he purchased two Avro 504 training aircraft. He had intended to establish a training school. He didn't say where, although I had hoped it could be here. He checked the land behind the new barn and said it meets the British aerodrome landing field requirements. Anyhow, as that is not to be, this is where you come in. The aircraft are in the new barn, still in crates. I would like you to give me your thoughts as to what I might do with them. I believe a qualified mechanic must assemble them before flight?'

Jimmy responded, 'Well, I'm amazed at what you have just said. Yes, a qualified mechanic must assemble aircraft and certify that they are fit for flight. It might surprise you, but as well as a pilot, I am a qualified mechanic permitted to certify Avro 504 aircraft. I was trained by the Avro Company. Sir, can I suggest after we finish tea, we see the aircraft?'

Mr Coles nodded, 'Yes, of course. I hope we haven't bored you, Jane.' She shook her head and smiled.

There were six large crates, three with wings and three with fuselages and three smaller crates with engines. Each crate had assembly and installation instructions.

Mr Coles had some farm hands open one of the wings crates and remove them. Jimmy was concerned if there had been any exposure to the elements causing water or heat damage. The packing had been done professionally. There was no damage, and the farmhands repacked the wings into the crate.

As they walked back to the office, both wondered where to go from there.

Jane suddenly asked, 'Jimmy could you assemble the aircraft here?'

Mr Coles, said excitedly, 'Yes, why not. That's why I built the new barn.'

Jimmy was trying to think quickly. He had the offer from England, but he couldn't do both. He needed long term security. He had two months before the other aircraft arrived. He turned to Mr Coles. 'I'll come over when I return from our honeymoon in about two weeks and start assembling one and take it from there. I will need the help of two men to do the lifting.'

Jane nodded, backing him up.

Mr Coles shook his hand. 'I'll pay you what you want.' He walked them to their gig and waved them goodbye.

They were both quiet on the way home. Jane let Jimmy think. He would talk when he was ready. She knew it was a big decision. Little did she know how big it was to be!

Jimmy was amazed that not only were two Avro aircraft in the district, but also a hangar and a potential airfield.

He started to think options. One – short term employment and two – long term employment. Three – the last option – would be to become a farmer. After delivering Jane back home and kissing her goodbye, he said, 'I'll see you tomorrow. I need to think about what's occurred today.' He waved and headed home.

After unharnessing the horse and stowing the gig and harness, he went to his room and collected a writing pad and a pencil. With a fresh cup of tea in hand, he sat out on the veranda. He drew two columns, one headed – Short, the other - Long.

Jimmy wanted to quietly consider both option – work for Avro or start a flying school.

Short term

Sparks Assemble aircraft and renew pilot licence.
Coles   Assemble aircraft only.

Sparks Project limited time?
Coles   Was he going to sell or keep the aircraft?

Sparks Contract
Coles   Handshake

Long term

Sparks Travel – where?
Coles   Become a flying instructor?

Sparks Be Avro Australian Representative?
Coles   Would he support a flying school on his land?

Sparks Employee
Coles   Contract

The big difference was the unknown travel destination and time away from home required by Avro, whereas the flying school would be near home.

Jane and he had been apart for so long, he was very reluctant to be apart again. Jimmy decided to visit Mr Coles by himself after he received an answer from Avro. He received the reply to his telegram the next day.

Hello Jimmy,

Thank you for your prompt response. I trust the following answers will be to your satisfaction.

1. *The project could last four to six months.*
2. *The travel would cover the capital cities on your east coast.*
3. *If we are successful in selling five or six aircraft, we would offer you employment, in Melbourne.*

Let me know your answer and I will advise of the place where the aircraft will be delivered and a contact name and address.

Regards – Sparks.

Jimmy now had a dilemma. He knew Avro's offer had long term potential. But could he have a preferred future near home with Mr Coles?

The following morning, he returned to Jane's. She was busy in the shearing shed, preparing it for the shearers returning next month. Jimmy showed Jane the answering telegram from Avro.

Jane said, predictably, 'I can't say I like the idea of you travelling interstate for unknown periods. We have spent too long apart. Enough is enough! What do you think?'

He replied, 'Yes, I agree. However, in the short term, I would like to assemble the aircraft in Melbourne. You could come to Melbourne with me, or I can come home at weekends and see where this offer takes me.'

Jane smiled. 'Yes, I can shop all day while you work. Seriously, I'd be happy with that arrangement.'

Jimmy said, 'Good. I have somewhere to start now. I'm off to visit Mr Coles. I have a proposition to put to him. I'll tell you about it on my way home.' He kissed her, then mounted his horse and trotted down the lane.

He was taking a chance on Mr Coles being home, with him being such a busy man in the community. Fortunately, he was home.

'Welcome. I didn't expect to see you so soon. Come in.'

After being shown to the parlour, Jimmy came straight to the point. 'Sir, I'd like to put a proposition to you. As you know, I'm a qualified aircraft mechanic and a pilot. I worked on and flew Avro 504 aircraft in England, France and the desert for nearly four years. You have two dual seater aircraft, a hangar and a possible airfield.'

He paused, took a deep breath and asked, 'Would you consider allowing me to set up a weekend pilot training centre and even joy flights with your facilities and aircraft. I feel sure we could come to some arrangement re contracts etc.'

He stopped and waited for Mr Coles' response.

Mr Coles stood up and walked to a window to look at the new hangar.

After a few minutes he returned and sat down. 'Yes, I like the idea. Can you make it work? Let me talk to some legal people and see where we would stand with the government. Obviously, there will be some act or regulation we would need to consider. I read somewhere the government was working on introducing air regulations based on the British system. I should have the answers when you come over to assemble the aircraft. You have made my day, young fellow.' They shook hands and Jimmy headed back to Jane's.

She was on the veranda with her mother having afternoon tea with jam and scones. After a few minutes, Jane's mother excused herself and left them to themselves.

Jimmy told Jane about the proposition he had put to Mr Coles and his response. It would be a solution to his employment concerns and his career.

Jane could see it resolving two potential major problems. He would be home, and he would be involved in his preferred career. She was delighted and felt sure Jimmy would be successful in this venture.

For the moment he was still a permanent army officer on eight weeks leave, but he now had an offer of two civilian jobs – assembling two aircraft locally and two or four aircraft at Melbourne, and the two jobs would not clash. He decided to only concentrate on the short term commitments for the next three months. At least, he would be doing what he enjoyed and be earning some money. His savings would not last forever.

The wedding day was getting closer and now took precedence. The women appeared to have everything under control. Then came an unexpected development.

A large truck crashed into the local hall a few days before the wedding and demolished the front of the building, rendering it unusable. There was no other building of similar size in the town.

Jane's mother panicked but Jane remembered Mr Coles barn. When she mentioned this, Ida spoke up,

'That's a good idea; he's my uncle. We can go and see him now. He should be home.'

Jane was delighted with this news. The two girls soon had a horse harnessed to a gig and were on their way to Mr Coles' homestead.

The two girls walked to the door and knocked. When no one came, Ida opened the door and walk in, calling out loudly, 'Uncle, where are you?'

A voice replied, 'I'm in the kitchen.'

Jane followed Ida, who approached her uncle and kissed him.

'Hello, and you, too, Jane. To what do I owe this pleasant surprise?'

Ida answered, 'Well, Jane is getting married and unfortunately, the hall was badly damaged last night, and we were wondering if we could use the new barn.'

Mr Coles said, 'First, let's go and see the extent of the damage to the hall.'

He called a farmhand and told him to harness a two-horse coach as soon as possible. Within twenty minutes the three of them were heading to town.

They headed straight to the hall, where a crowd was standing around chatting.

When Mr Coles approached with the two girls, several men said 'hello' to him. He walked around the council barriers and called to one of the bystanders to come over. They looked closely at the damage and spoke quietly to each other. Mr Coles came over and told the girls to go to the town café for half an hour and wait for him. The two men then went to the shire office to speak with the engineer.

Half an hour later he returned, smiling. 'The council believe it can be repaired in time for your wedding.'

Jane kissed him, saying, 'You're a miracle worker,' and started to cry.

Mr Coles drove the girls back for their gig. They each waved goodbye.

Jane could hardly wait to tell her mother what had occurred in town. She was delighted.

True to their word the council appointed a contractor who completed the rebuild of the hall the night prior to the wedding. It still had a fresh paint smell but with eucalyptus sprayed on at the entrance surround, the smell was minimal.

The rehearsal took two attempts due to Andrew's nervousness. He dropped the wedding ring, and it took them ten minutes to find it. It had rolled back under the church seats.

On the way home they checked on the flowers. Would they be delivered on time? The answer was "Yes". They then visited the caterers. The answer was the same "Yes".

Jimmy visited the major and asked, 'Is tomorrow's Guard organised?'

The major laughed. 'It's normal to be nervous before a wedding. Don't worry, everything will be professionally performed.' He walked Jimmy to the door. 'Relax, go home and have a beer or two.'

The big day arrived. The planning had been successful. Even the weather was fine, no wind and plenty of sunshine. The bridal coach looked splendid with the new coat of paint and seat covers. It had two matching black horses with polished black harnesses, completing the picture.

Ida had arrived at Jane's the previous day and stayed overnight. Likewise, Andrew stayed at Jimmy's farm.

The bride's parents would travel with Jane, and Jimmy's parents with him and Andrew. Andrew and Ida would go home with their parents and Jane's parents would drive to the Symons' home.

Jimmy was dressed in uniform complete with medals and sword on his left hip. Andrew was dressed in grey tails and top hat, looking every inch an aristocratic gentleman.

The women were in a flap, chatting excitedly and very happy. Jane and Ida were tended by the older women who helped them dress and then groomed by the local hairdresser. Jane's father was dressed similarly to Andrew. He was downstairs and sat relaxed, drinking a beer while listening to the horse races in Melbourne.

After a glance at the wall clock, Mr Hay stood up and called, 'Time to go.' It was five minutes early, but he didn't want to be blamed for arriving late at the church. Amid some last minute nerves from the women, he firmly ushered them into the coach.

The Guardsmen arrived early and tethered their horses behind the church. Those who were not ushers, sat in the rear seats holding their hats and swords on their laps. They would need to exit quickly at the end of the service to form up as the Honour Guard.

The church seats were soon occupied. Many were not guests but what better way could a country town's residents enjoy a Saturday afternoon, than to dress up and see a wedding. Although most of them were women, a few men were dragged along.

Jimmy and Andrew drove to the church and arrived five minutes early, looking very smart – Jimmy in uniform and Andrew resplendent in his formal suit. Andrew was nervous and it needed Jimmy to calm him. The families were already in the church and were chatting to each other.

The priest came over and approached the groom and best man, asking, 'Are you both prepared for your roles and do you have the ring safely in your pocket, Andrew?'

Andrew laughed. 'Oh, yes, indeed I do.' They each looked towards the church doorway where some activity was occurring.

A young boy excitedly ran up to the organist. 'I can see their coach coming.' The organist had been quietly playing a variety of popular songs. She stopped and was ready to play the bridal tune.

The bridal coach stopped opposite the pathway to the church doorway. Mr Hay helped the bride and the bridesmaid to alight. The small boy was standing in the doorway and now waved to the organist, who started to play. The church gathering all stood for a good view, as the bridal party entered the church, with four flower girls following them.

There were plenty of quiet words of praise being used for her gown. Mr Hay was beaming with happiness, proud for his daughter at this moment.

Jimmy and Andrew were looking back at them walking up the aisle. Jane looked radiant in her dress and her beautiful hair showing beneath her veil.

The moment had arrived. They stood alongside each other and smiling, looked into each other's face, seeing their love for each other. The priest commenced the formalities. All was going well until the priest embarrassingly had the hiccups. Trying to look serious was difficult, for all and sundry, including the bride and groom. Between the hiccing and cupping the formalities were completed by the embarrassed priest. Andrew made sure the ring was available on call. Amid claps and cheers the bridal party happily waved as they walked from the church.

Immediately the service was completed, the Honour Guard quickly donned their hats attached their swords and formed two lines outside the church door. Swords were drawn and raised for the bridal party to pass under. The local photographer took several photos of the Honour Guard and then of the bride and groom and guests. The Guard of Honour then mounted their horses and escorted the bridal party to the local hall for the reception. The street pedestrians waved and shouted good wishes. Some young larrikins shouted a few words of lewd advice, typical of farm boys who had grown up with breeding livestock. Jane and Jimmy just smiled.

When they arrived at the reception, a young stable hand took the coach out to the stables and removed the "Just married" sign.

The reception room was immaculate with newly painted walls and satin drapes. The tables were adorned with flowers and glitter, giving the room an appropriate gala affair.

During the pre-drinks, Jane and Jimmy circulated with the guests thanking them for coming to the wedding. The table by the entry gradually filled with presents. Andrew had the task of collecting them and taking them to Jimmy's home.

Dinner was a typical country menu – corn soup, an ample selection of vegetables, roast beef or chicken with a bread roll. Desert was ice cream and jelly or apple pie and custard. Drinks were beer, wine or soft drinks.

Jimmy and Jane sat quietly holding hands, while enjoying listening to the happy chatter of their quests.

Andrew stood up and tapped the side of his glass. The guests gave him their attention. Speech time had arrived. Andrew spoke with his best lawyer voice – clear and measured.

He told a few childhood stories about Jimmy and Jane, that even their parents didn't know! What little he knew of Jimmy's military career, he related. He then spoke of Jane. Of his admiration for her, particularly of her love for Jimmy during their long separation.

He had a few telegrams; most were congratulatory. One was an old well-known quote. "Take it from one who knows, tie your nightdress to your toes." signed "Aunt Jean". She had twelve children – all girls. Two telegrams he wouldn't read out. He handed them to Jimmy, who glanced at them and didn't hand them back. He appreciated the telegrams but some humour was not for mixed company. Andrew then called the guests to be upstanding and 'Toast the Bride and Groom'. A few more toasts and Andrew sat down.

It was now Jimmy's turn to respond. He commenced by thanking Andrew for his support during the wedding day and Ida and the flower girls. Next, he thanked their parents for their organising skills and the council for their prompt repairs to the hall. Jimmy then turned to Jane and took her hand and helped her stand up alongside him. He said, 'On behalf of Jane and I, we thank you for making this such a memorable day. Enjoy yourselves and have a safe trip home. Thank you.'

The band started up with a slow waltz. Jimmy led Jane onto the dance floor and started the bridal waltz.

After a lap of the floor, Jimmy waved the guests to join in dancing.

An hour later, Jane said, 'I'm exhausted. Let's leave.'

Jimmy agreed and asked Andrew to tell the guests they were leaving in five minutes. The guests lined up for their departure and after many kisses and handshakes, they climbed into their coach and drove home to change. They then headed to the next town where he had booked a room for the night. It would be dark when they arrived. Tomorrow they would go to Melbourne by train for a week and leave the coach at the hotel.

After they checked in at the hotel, they decided to have a drink before retiring. They were sitting quietly in a corner, when Jane said, 'I hope I don't disappoint you.'

Jimmy replied, 'Strange you should say that. That's what I'm thinking about me. Maybe not tonight. Let's have a good sleep and wait until tomorrow. As you once said, we've waited this long what's another day!'

Jane kissed him.

When they went to bed, they undressed in front of each other without any embarrassment. Although Jimmy jumped into bed quickly when he saw Jane's breasts. Jane laughed at him as she saw his manhood rising. They kissed and lay together with Jimmy fondling her breasts. However, he managed to control his desire.

Jane started to cry. She told Jimmy she was so happy, but her pent up emotions had caught up to her. They went to sleep cuddled together.

After showering, they enjoyed breakfast and were driven to the station by the owner of the hotel. Jimmy had booked first class seats and they were well looked after by the train staff. The day was sunny and dry. They sat there holding hands, enjoying the passing scenery.

Jimmy remembered two important previous train trips – the first going to England with his Uncle Michael and the second, returning home after the war.

He laughed and said, 'I've had three train trips and each one has been a turning point in my life.' When he explained them to Jane, she nodded in agreement.

He had booked a penthouse room at the Metropole opposite Parliament House. It had extensive views of Melbourne overlooking the river, several grand buildings and in the distance was Government House with its large gardens. They decided to explore Melbourne town the next day and asked the receptionist to arrange a Hansom cab for the morning. *[NOTE 4]*

After dinner they retired to their room somewhat apprehensively. After showering they went to bed.

Jimmy had thought of this moment for a long time. He kissed her gently and she responded. After undressing her, and himself, he gazed at her naked body. She was a beautiful woman who had kept her figure trim with her physical work as a farmer's daughter. Her breasts were firm, and she had a flat abdomen. He started to caress her breasts and back.

She responded and soon submitted. Her first time was extraordinarily satisfying. She felt pleasure throughout her body and clung tightly to Jimmy for some time afterwards.

He looked down at her enquiringly.

She said, 'I had no need to worry. It was uncomfortable at first, but it was delightful.'

He kissed her. 'I love you more each moment.'

She would never forget the night she lost her virginity.

The following morning a telegram was delivered to their room from his father. It contained the words of a telegram from Avro.

When next in Melbourne, contact Mr Alan Eden of AIR CONSTRUCTIONS at Point Cook. This is an Australian Government owned airfield. The two Avro 504s are stowed in one of their hangars. He is expecting your contact. Please advise state of disassembled aircraft i.e. water or other damage. Signed Mr Sharp.

He handed the telegram to Jane, who asked, 'Where's Point Cook?'

He replied, 'I think it's about an hour west from Melbourne.'

Jane said, 'Well let's do our sightseeing today and worry about the telegram tomorrow.'

Jimmy nodded and said, 'Let's go.'

The Hansom cab arrived on time and away they went to explore the attractions of Melbourne. The cab driver had been born in Melbourne in 1880 and had not left the city. He was affable without being overpowering and he really knew its history. From his high seat behind the cab, he relayed the information through the open roof panel.

They crossed over the main bridge and visited the beautiful gardens around the Governor's House. Then down to the beach and back along the river. The city had many impressive buildings, not unlike those he had seen in the UK. The day passed quickly, and they arrived back at the hotel around sundown, tired but happy.

They approached the hotel desk and asked the attendant, 'Where is Point Cook and how can we get there?'

They were advised, 'Go by train to Laverton Station. It is around an hour trip as it stops several times at other stations on the way. You need further transport to get to Point Cook. I can arrange a train booking for you if you wish for tomorrow.'

Jimmy replied, 'Yes, please do, and let me know as soon as you have done the booking. We'll be in our room.'

The attendant called within ten minutes advising them they were booked on the train and would arrive at eleven o'clock.

Jimmy wrote a telegram addressed to Mr Alan Eden.

My wife and I will arrive eleven hundred hours at Laverton Station. Please answer urgently if you can meet us.' signed Captain J. Symons M.C.'

The answer was quick. *Yes, will meet you. Signed Alan Eden.*

The train trip was a surprise. They had not realised how spread out the suburbs of Melbourne had become. Laverton was a small fringe town.

Jimmy and Jane alighted and stood together to help Alan Eden identify them.

A short time later, a tall man approached them. 'Am I addressing Mr and Mrs Symons?'

Jimmy offered his hand. 'Yes, you are, and you're Mr Eden, I presume.'

He nodded and said, 'Welcome to Laverton. I have a car. Point Cook is only ten minutes away.'

Point Cook had been an active airfield during WW1. It was now being used for a variety of aviation purposes – military and civil. Mr Eden was the managing director of Air Constructions and had hired a hangar. They went to his office to talk about how the AVRO 504 reassemblies would occur.

Alan started the discussion. 'The crates are open for your inspection. But first, can you give me an estimate of how long it will take to assemble both aircraft?'

Jimmy answered, 'That would depend on what manpower is available to assist me. I would require several competent general mechanics to be able to completely assemble both aircraft ready for flight within ten to twelve days. They would both require to be test flown. As you no doubt know, both aircraft are still on the British Register, and I am licensed to issue a maintenance release.'

Alan replied, 'Yes, I am aware of your qualifications and your request to revalidate your pilot's licence. Manpower should not be a problem. Many locals are ex-WW1 aircraft mechanics. I have interviewed ten already. They can start when you're ready.'

Jimmy was unprepared for this statement. He needed to think and discuss it with Jane, who had sat listening to every word.

Alan interrupted Jimmy's thoughts. 'We have visitors VIP living quarters here. Can I suggest you stay here for tonight and we will talk more tomorrow?' At that moment a polite tap sounded on Alan's office door. It was Alan's wife.

'Hello, you arrive at an opportune moment. This is Helen, my wife. Meet Jane and Jimmy Symons, here for discussions regarding the new aircraft.'

After greetings were exchanged. Alan suggested he and Jimmy visit the hangar, and Helen show Jane the VIP quarters and the officers' mess. He was hoping to impress Jane, who would encourage Jimmy to stay the night. Jane and Helen then left the office.

The men went to the hangar. It was large enough to accommodate six or so Avro 504's. The crates had the tops and sides removed but the contents were still anchored to their bases.

After an hour-long inspection by Jimmy, he nodded to Alan and said, 'Excellent. There is no water or other damage to the aircraft parts, the propellors or the engines. Can you advise Mr Sparks? He'll be pleased.' He sat on a chair at a long table and opened a box of documents. They contained the aircraft log books and maintenance data. He laid out some unfolded diagrams. They nearly covered the entire table. He turned to Alan and said, 'Everything is here, including the tools and jigs.'

Alan then asked the question, 'When can you start assembling the aircraft?'

Jimmy said, 'Can we talk about this over a cup of tea?'

Alan and Jimmy went to the officers' mess and found Jane and Helen already there.

Helen said, 'I've shown Jane the VIP accommodation. She likes it.'

Jimmy looked at Jane, waiting for her to comment.

Jane said, 'We're in Melbourne already and we're already planning to stay for a few days. The accommodation is excellent, so if you want us to remain for a few days I'm happy to, but we need our clothes from Melbourne.'

Alan interrupted, 'Jimmy, I can send a vehicle to Melbourne for your clothes now, if you wish to stay.'

Jimmy nodded, 'I'll have to start the project eventually. Why not tomorrow?'

Alan replied, 'Splendid. Now, excuse me. I have men to organise, clothes to collect and a telegram to send. Helen, can you escort our visitors to the accommodation and arrange dinner for four at the mess this evening? I'll meet you then. Bye for now.'

When Jimmy and Jane entered the house, the first thing they did was to take off their shoes, and then lay down on the bed. They had found the day long and demanding; both were tired. Not surprisingly, they dozed for a short time.

After waking, they sat down to discuss the day's events. Jimmy advised Jane he would not know how long it would take to assemble an aircraft until he saw how his mechanic assistants performed. Hopefully, six days or less.

Alan and Helen arrived when it was time for dinner and escorted them to the mess. During pre-dinner drinks, he met two pilots who had served in the desert.

They had heard of him and his rescue exploit. 'How did you do it?'

Reluctantly, he told them the story, emphasising how lucky he had been.

The dinner gong sounded. He excused himself and rejoined Jane. The evening was enjoyable. Good food and good company. When they arrived back at the accommodation, their clothes from Melbourne had been delivered. An early night saw them kissing and cuddling again, leading to the ultimate.

Next morning after breakfast, Helen called for Jane in a gig and advised Jimmy they were off to the beach for a picnic.

Jimmy was now about to become a pioneer member of the Australian aviation industry.

CHAPTER EIGHT

The Decision

Alan and Jimmy walked to the hangar, where ten workers were waiting.

Jimmy asked, 'How many of you have worked on an airplane and for how long?' He selected seven who had at least a year's experience.

Firstly, Jimmy measured out an area on the hangar floor, the width and length of the Avro 504K. He then had three men set up the jigs. The other four men were to unbolt the fuselage from the floor of the crate and carry it to the jigs. Jimmy carefully positioned the fuselage onto the jigs, double checking the measurements. Next came the lower wings to be positioned onto their jigs. After shifting the wings to and fro, the bolt holes on the fuselage and wings were lined up and the bolts were fitted and tightened. He allowed the men to go home early.

Jimmy stayed to double check measurements in accordance with the instructions. When he was satisfied with his figures, he went to Alan's office to update him. 'I think I could complete this aircraft in five days. Today's progress has been excellent.'

The next morning the men were waiting for Jimmy. He thought, *That's good. They're really keen.*

One mechanic came over and asked Jimmy if would he mind signing their maintenance experience log after the aircraft were assembled. 'Yes certainly, I'd be delighted.'

Today they would install the top wing and the eight struts. This was very time consuming. Aligning the wing to the fuselage was easy but installation of the struts was frustrating. Eventually all eight were bolted into the wing brackets. The undercarriage was fitted last while the aircraft was still on the jigs. Jimmy stayed back and again checked the dimensions and angles as per the diagrams.

Then came the rigging of the straining or bracing wires. It was tedious and laborious. It required checking and rechecking the tensions. Eventually the tasks were completed, and the team sat down and looked at the assembled airframe with satisfaction. At the end of the third day, they removed the jigs.

Two of the mechanics had worked on engines before. He assigned them to install the engine into the engine mounts and connect the various hoses, pipes and control cables as instructed in the maintenance manual. He monitored their work and found them most capable. The other mechanics installed the fuel tank, connected the flight cables and some minor items. Jimmy got involved with the rigging of the flight cables and had an experienced former sergeant mechanic, Ian Miles, double check his work.

By the middle of the fourth day, only the propellor needed to be fitted and the engine ground run and tuned. Hopefully, he could taxi it the next day and, maybe, have it test flown the same day.

While Jimmy was working, Helen and Jane went to Melbourne for some shopping and sightseeing. Another time she went to a women's luncheon and met the Governor's wife. Jane now had bragging rights.

Over breakfast they discussed the previous day's events. They couldn't at dinner, as they were always in the company of others. Jimmy was content to stay just so long as Jane was happy. Fortunately, Jane and Helen enjoyed each other's company.

The fifth day was abuzz with excitement. The word had got around that the Avro 504 was ready to fly. Not really, but close to.

The propellor had been fitted, the engine controls rigging double checked and the fuel tank was filled.

The aircraft was pushed from the hangar amid cheers from the onlookers. Jimmy primed the fuel system, climbed into the cockpit and selected the magnetos to "on" and selected fuel "on"' and then gave the mechanic the thumbs up.

The mechanic pulled the propellor to a compression position and then pulled the propellor a half turn. Nothing happened. It took two more attempts before the engine roared into life, enveloping the aircraft in exhaust smoke for a few seconds.

Jimmy checked the oil pressure gauge and allowed the engine to warm. He then waved the mechanics to remove the wheel chocks.

The aircraft rolled forward until Jimmy slowly opened the throttle and increased the speed to a fast-walking pace. He headed to the open area used for take-off and landing. When he reached the airfield perimeter, he turned the aircraft into the wind and then opened the throttle fully. The aircraft responded immediately.

He held the control stick central and continued until he felt the tail lift and the aircraft rose a few feet. Jimmy then retarded the throttle and the aircraft settled back onto the ground. He taxied back to the hangar and the waiting crowd.

He closed the throttle and switched the magnetos to off, well before where the spectators were standing.

The mechanics soon had the aircraft chocked. He stepped from the aircraft to be greeted by Alan, who jokingly said, 'I thought you were stealing the aircraft. What do you think – is everything as you expected?'

Jimmy nodded. 'I think it's ready for a test flight now. I have a few checks to do first.' He called the mechanics over. 'I want every wing attachment, the bracing wires and strut nuts and bolts checked for security. If you find one loose, tell me. Also, check the engine mounting bolts are tight.'

Jimmy watched them as they checked every bracing wire, nut and bolt. They were all found to be in accordance with installation instructions. He then carried out a second inspection of the aircraft fuselage and wings and opened the engine cowl for a quick look. The final task was to measure the tightness of the control cables with a tensiometer. Satisfied the aircraft was serviceable for flight, Jimmy was now ready to certify the maintenance documents.

Alan had organised an Australian military pilot to test fly the aircraft.

Lunch time in the mess was noisy, with an air of excitement in the room. Jimmy had received several handshakes and thumbs up for a job well done.

After a long lunch, they went to the hangar to await the test pilot. Alan told Jimmy he was a former British Royal Flying Corps squadron leader, who had transferred to the Australian Army as an advisor on aviation matters. The Australian Government was in the middle of establishing a Royal Australian Air Force and he was heavily involved in the manpower structure process.

'Ah, there he is. Over here, John.' Alan waved. 'Jimmy, meet Squadron Leader John Ford and John meet Captain Jimmy Symons, semi-retired.

John smiled. 'I heard of you when I was at the Avro headquarters last year. Good to meet you. I believe you know all there is to know about the Avro 504.'

Jimmy laughed. 'Well, I know a little.'

John examined the maintenance documents and then inspected the aircraft. He asked, 'Have you taxied it yet?'

Jimmy replied, 'Yes, I took it to take-off speed and it handled as expected. I felt like taking off, but my pilot's licence needs revalidating, so I obeyed the law and resisted the urge.'

John laughed. 'We can talk about that later, but first I'm going flying.'

The engine started at the second effort and with a quick wave, John taxied to the far end of the airfield and turned into the wind. The crowd watched as the aircraft accelerated and slowly climbed, heading into the distance.

A few minutes later the aircraft reappeared and steadily climbed for five minutes and then turned slowly to the left and then to the right and then level.

John repeated the turns only much more tightly. His next movement was a roll and then he climbed and deliberately slowed the aircraft until it stalled. As the aircraft began spinning, John pushed the nose down and centred the control column. Slowly the wings stopped turning and the aircraft assumed a normal flying attitude as he pulled the control column back and levelled the aircraft. John then landed and taxied to the hangar.

Jimmy waited patiently for John to come over.

John nodded. 'It handles very well. The stall recovery surprised me; it was easy and quick. Well done, Jimmy. Let's have a beer and a chat.'

Alan drove them to the mess and sat with them. He needed to send a report to the UK with their comments and advise that they had assembled an Avro 504 and had it test flown in five days.

John asked, 'I was surprised that there was so little swing on take-off. Why is this?'

Jimmy replied, 'When I was working in the technical department, I found the majority of ground mishaps were occurring during take-off and landing. When I began flying, I gave this matter some thought and came up with the idea to bias the rudder a few degrees to counter the propellor wash. I submitted the idea to the War Department, but it took twelve months to reach the correct department, then the war was over the following month. End of story. No one's interested in modifications to aircraft now. I also wrote a report on the differences in the lift capabilities between a long narrow wing and a short stubby one, such as in vogue now. They're only interested in selling them now, with so many sitting idle.'

John said. 'I'm not surprised. Bureaucracy is hard to bypass. Now I've been advised by Avro that they agreed to help you validate your pilot's licence and you're probably not surprised to learn I have been given that task. If you wish, we can start your validation on Saturday. I'm staying for some tests with the local flying school over the weekend.'

On the morning of the fifth day, Alan asked if Jimmy's team could start assembling the second aircraft.

Jimmy agreed. He had Sergeant Miles select four men to start setting up the jigs. Jimmy needed the two others to assist him with the aircraft handling.

So, by the end of the fifth day, the first aircraft had been certified fit for flight and had been test flown, plus the assembly of the second aircraft had started. Alan Eden was delighted and immediately informed Avro UK of the current status of the project.

That evening, Alan organised a formal dinner for local dignitaries and businessmen to celebrate the dawn of an Australian aviation Industry.

Saturday heralded a new day, sunshine with little cloud. Jane knew Jimmy was apprehensive, but she felt once he was airborne he would be confident and relaxed. Sergeant Miles had the aircraft fuelled and ready to fly. John sat with Jimmy as he answered a few questions on airmanship and safety issues.

'I want you to do a few turns, two take-offs and landings and a tail stall. I have an hour navigation exercise for you to carry out this afternoon. Agreed?'

Jimmy nodded!

After a preflight inspection, Jimmy climbed into the cockpit. He moved the control column around, confirming the controls were free.

The engine started on the second attempt and, after allowing the engine to warm, he checked the oil pressure was normal. He waved the chocks away and taxied to the perimeter, heading into the wind.

Jimmy felt alive as he pushed the throttle forward. The aircraft powered away and soon reached take-off speed. The tail lifted and, with a slight backward movement of the control column, the aircraft rose from the airfield. He maintained a climb angle but kept flying straight. When he reached an altitude of two thousand feet, he levelled and turned the aircraft to the left and then to the right. He now felt comfortable and confident to do some tight turns and dives. The aircraft was a delight to fly.

He climbed to three thousand feet and was ready to perform a stall. He pulled the nose up and the throttle back and waited until the airspeed could no longer support the aircraft. The aircraft shuddered and slowly fell from the sky. It soon began spinning. Jimmy centred the control column and pushed the nose down to increase airspeed and waited for the spinning to slowly stop. He then slowly pulled up the nose while opening the engine throttle to cruise speed. With the aircraft now stable. Jimmy flew back to the airfield and carried out two touch and goes and then landed. *[NOTE 5]*

After he closed the throttle, the mechanics chocked the wheels and helped him alight. John walked over and greeted him with a thumbs up and a smile. 'Your recovery from the stall was textbook standard. Do you still want to do your Navex today?'

Jimmy nodded. 'Definitely. It's a good day for flying.'

John laid out a military ordinance map on the desk. 'I want you to fly to the Ballarat Racecourse. There is a horse racing meeting there this afternoon.'

He pointed, 'I want you to drop two flour bombs in the centre of the of the course, obviously not during a race. Have you been there before?'

Jimmy shook his head. 'No, I've heard of it.'

John continued. 'It's a large town west from here.' He continued, 'I then want you to fly south to Geelong and fly down the main street twice and then return.'

He paused, 'I want you to draft a flight plan, giving your compass headings and check points en route, estimated speed, including today's wind component and your selected altitude. There is a white painted line over past the hangar. Check your compass accuracy by straddling this line. This line is a north–south compass check point. Most compasses have a one to two degrees error. Compare your reading and record the difference on your flight plan.

'One error reading for zero degrees north and another error reading for one eighty degrees south. I'm aware you probably know everything I've said, but as an examiner I am required to brief you as such.'

Jimmy replied, 'I understand, and it will probably refresh the brain cells.'

The flight was planned to take-off just after lunch. The flight plan took about half an hour to complete. Jimmy studied the map and recorded a direct compass heading to Ballarat and then added a new heading, to the north, to the racecourse. He also identified two towns en route to confirm his course. Ballarat was fifteen hundred feet above sea level, so he decided on a cruise altitude of four thousand feet. The flight distance was approximately one hundred and seventy miles round trip. He would cruise at a speed of seventy miles per hour, this was an estimated flight time of two hours. The aircraft, with a full fuel tank of twenty five imperial gallons had a cruise range of two hundred and fifty to three hundred miles. The weather forecast was for clear skies and no clouds and winds from the west up to ten m.p.h. He showed the flight plan to John, who just nodded and said, 'Away you go.'

Jimmy wore his military issue watch from those heady days. After starting and warming the engine, he taxied out to the airfield white line to check his compass accuracy.

John yelled to him, 'Stay away from clouds. Turn back if you don't feel comfortable.' The compass revealed an error of minus one degree on both the north and south readings, which was acceptable. He headed the aircraft into the wind and slowly opened the throttle.

The tail lifted, and at forty knots, he pulled back on the control column and the aircraft started to climb. At three hundred feet, he turned the aircraft to the flight plan heading, direct to Ballarat. He continued to climb to four thousand feet, levelled out and set the throttle to cruise engine speed. He anticipated he would arrive over Ballarat at approximately fourteen hundred hours.

The countryside was a typical Australian scene. Below was like a green carpet, dotted with farm buildings and livestock.

He noticed the road to Geelong was skirted by a railway line. After twenty minutes a town appeared ahead. He identified it as Bacchus Marsh. He was on course and on time.

The second check point, Ballan, was on his port side and abeam of him. He slightly adjusted his heading. The westerly wind had blown him marginally off course. The countryside was again dotted with small farms and green paddocks with livestock grazing contentedly.

Ballarat appeared slightly off to his right. He started to descend to five hundred feet. The westerly wind had pushed him a mile or two off his initial heading. He flew over the main street, a wide double road with a centre strip of trees. It was now time to follow his new heading north to the racecourse. Within ten minutes, he spotted it directly ahead. He descended to two hundred feet and commenced a long low approach.

A race had just been completed as he flew over the boundary fence. He released a flour bomb in the middle of the racecourse. As it exploded into a white cloud, the race goers applauded. They had been advised of an aircraft bombing exercise.

Jimmy looked back and saw the faces looking up at him, waving. He then turned one eighty degrees and repeated another bombing run, dropping another flour bomb. He waggled his wings to the crowd and then turned on a direct heading to Geelong and began climbing to three thousand feet.

Cloud was appearing ahead, but it was mostly high, with only a few small scattered low clouds. They were not of concern. His timing was only a few minutes behind his estimate.

Jimmy believed that as he was now flying direct to Geelong, he would make up the lost time on the way back to base. The miles rolled along, with Meridith, his check point, appearing as per his flight plan. He was relaxed and enjoying the Navex. Eventually he could see the waters of Corio Bay dead ahead with Geelong looming closer. He lowered the nose and levelled out at five hundred feet. He flew over the town, down the main street and returned to repeat the low flight. He now set a compass heading to Point Cook.

The course back to Point Cook aligned Jimmy with a main road and a railway line on his left. With clear skies, it was impossible to get lost. The engine was running smoothly. He was singing a popular tune. About ten minutes from his forecast arrival at Point Cook, he was given a wakeup call when, out of nowhere, an unexpected rain squall shook the aircraft. It was only light with a few bumps and soon ended.

Jimmy was annoyed he hadn't seen it coming from his right side. He soon identified Point Cook and commenced his descent. The landing was smooth. As he taxied to the hangar, he felt a sense of accomplishment and pride. His flight time was within five minutes of his predicted time.

Being a Saturday, a small curious crowd greeted him with waving arms and applause. He kissed Jane and held her hand. He then shook hands with John and Alan.

John spoke first. 'Almost right on your estimated time of arrival. Well done. I'm happy to validate your licence.'

After changing, he joined them for dinner at the mess. He spent the first twenty minutes answering aviation questions before Jane interrupted and said, 'Let's change to a subject which women can join in.'

Helen nodded in agreement. Alan took the hint and asked the women, 'How did the Geelong shops compare to Melbourne's shops?' The evening was enjoyable and finished early.

Jimmy welcomed the early night.

Lying in bed, Jane put her arms around him. 'I'm so proud of you', then kissed him goodnight.

Sunday, the four of them went to the small military church where the minister spoke of the evils of war. John was not available as he was required by the aeroclub to train potential new pilots. Alan commandeered a base vehicle and they drove to the Werribee River for a picnic and a spot of fishing. The weather was sunny and windless. It was a complete break from aircraft, even if it was only a day. No fish were caught and each of them ended up with a sunburnt face.

Monday was a briefing day from Sergeant Miles. He reported the parts had all been removed from the crates and then set up and the fuselage had been set onto the jigs. They were now ready to attach the lower wings. This was successfully carried out. A drama occurred when they went to attach the upper wings and they were unable to locate the attach bolts. They had been ticked off as having been in the crates. After an hour of fruitless search, Jimmy decided to fit the undercarriage while he considered his options.

Fortunately, when a mechanic climbed into the cockpit to insert the undercarriage attach bolts, he found the lost bolts on the floor of the cockpit. There was a huge sigh of relief from all. These bolts were specially manufactured and not available off the shelf. The aircraft assembly now proceeded at a surprising rate. Tuesday went according to plan. By Wednesday midday they were ready to carry out the engine run.

The engine ground running took more time than expected. It took over an hour to tune. The fuel system was causing it to run too rich. After dismantling, cleaning and reassembling a few components, the engine finally ran smoothly.

John successfully carried out the test flight to finally complete the Melbourne Avro project. Alan telegrammed England with the good news that the project had been completed well within the two weeks anticipated.

That evening a farewell dinner was held with a few speeches and several celebratory drinks.

Alan had managed his project on time and Jimmy had his British pilot's licence revalidated. He had been advised by a representative of the Australian Defence Department that both his British Aircraft Maintenance Licence and his British Pilot's Licence would be recognised by the imminent Australian Navigation Act and Regulations.

Jane and Jimmy embarked by train to Melbourne the following morning. Alan and Helen, together with John, Sergeant Miles and his team of mechanics farewelled them.

True to his word, Jimmy had signed each mechanic's maintenance logbook. He had made many friends at Laverton.

Jane wanted to stay in Melbourne to do some shopping, so they returned to the Metropole Hotel to stay overnight. He was pleasantly surprised to receive a telegram from Mr Sparks advising him a payment had been telegraphed to his bank account.

Jane said, 'Wow! That's a lot of money!'

It even surprised Jimmy. He said to Jane, 'Since you have had your honeymoon interrupted, buy whatever dress you wish.'

She replied, 'You can come with me and help me select it.'

That afternoon Jimmy was dragged from shop to shop. Finally, Jane found her dress. The next day they travelled to Mylonga. Home at last.

CHAPTER NINE

A Successful Career

After a day lounging around the farm, Jimmy went to visit Mr Coles. A farm hand said he was in the new barn.

He waved as he saw Jimmy coming. 'How was Melbourne?'

Jimmy replied, 'Too busy for me. I thought I should come and tell you what I've been up to.'

Mr Coles motioned him to sit down alongside him.

Jimmy continued, 'I was advised by AVRO that the crates with the aircraft had arrived and was asked when I could start assembling them. As I was already in Melbourne, Jane and I went to Point Cook. To cut a long story short, both aircraft were assembled, and test flown in ten working days. Also, I have had my pilot's licence revalidated. I've not heard from AVRO since, so I'd like to plan to assemble your aircraft.'

Mr Coles was smiling and said, 'I was a bit concerned there for a minute. Yes, draft me a plan and tell me what you need. Then we can talk some more.'

Jimmy agreed it was time to start assembling the aircraft.

Jimmy's plan needed at least four persons with at least some mechanical knowledge. The timeframe would be at least six days per aircraft. He wondered if Sergeant Miles would be interested in coming up to assist him in overseeing the assembling of the two aircraft.

Also, he needed to be able to get John Ford to come up and test fly the aircraft. As Jimmy would be certifying the aircraft fit for flight, he felt it was improper to test fly the planes as well. He telegraphed Alan and asked him if he could release Sergeant Miles for two weeks to assist him. A prompt answer was, *Yes, send me the details and I'll make it happen.*

Mr Coles looked at his plan and nodded. 'I can provide two farm hands with mechanical experience and two others who are intelligent. With your sergeant and yourself, would they suit you?'

Jimmy replied, 'Yes, I'd like to start next Monday.' They shook hands and Jimmy headed to town and sent a telegram to Alan asking if Sergeant Miles could arrive the next Sunday. He then went to have lunch whilst awaiting an answer. When confirmation arrived he headed home, content with the day's results.

Jane and Jimmy met Sergeant Miles and drove him to Mr Coles farm, where it had been arranged he would stay during the project.

After introducing him to Mr Coles, and some of his farm hands, they returned home.

Monday started with a hive of activity. Marking an area for the jigs and setting them up was the first task. Then came the complete removal of the major aircraft components from the crates and checking that the minor items were all there. By midday they were ready to place the fuselage onto the jigs.

Sergeant Miles was happy with his new team up to now and hoped their enthusiasm would continue. By the day's end, the lower wings had been bolted into place and the struts and wires laid out ready for the next day's upper wing installation.

The next three days saw the aircraft ready. Sergeant Miles and Jimmy made a good pair, and the farm helpers were more than capable of performing mechanical tasks under direction.

On the fifth day, the engine run was carried out successfully. That afternoon John arrived to perform the test flight. The aircraft performed as expected, and without any mechanical defects. Mr Coles was delighted that the aircraft was assembled within the planned time and without any problems. After the test flight, John invited Mr Coles to fly with him for ten minutes over his property and the town. Initially hesitant, he eventually agreed. After a short briefing, John and Mr Coles took off.

There was no cloud and Mr Coles soon recognised local roads and farms. Flying over the town, he identified the town landmarks. He was surprised how different they appeared from the air. The flight was soon completed, and Mr Coles excitedly waved as they taxied back to the hangar. There was still another aircraft to assemble.

The following Monday was a repeat of the previous week. Except the engine run was carried out late on the afternoon of the fourth day. The previous week's experience had improved their skills and understanding of the associated assembly tasks and had made them most competent. John had stayed in town some nights; other nights he dined at Mr Coles' farm and stayed overnight there.

The aircraft had a pre-flight inspection and was refuelled. John started up the engine and with a wave headed out to the far paddock fence. Opening his throttle, he sped down the grass paddock and, as normal practice, continued flying in a straight line until out of sight. When the aircraft did not reappear as expected within ten minutes, Jimmy felt something was wrong. After waiting for twenty minutes, he knew something had happened.

He immediately called Sergeant Miles over and told him to push out the other Avro 504 to preflight and fuel it. 'You and I are going flying as soon as the aircraft is ready.' Within twenty minutes they were airborne. They flew straight as John had. After seeing nothing for ten minutes. Jimmy turned ninety degrees for five minutes, still finding nothing. He then reversed his course for ten minutes.

Then the sergeant yelled, 'To the left near the river.' There was the aircraft intact. John waved to them, holding up a fuel can. He had landed on a river flat where the river had meandered for many centuries. Jimmy flew low and waggled his wings to acknowledge he had seen him. He then climbed to two thousand feet and, when he could see the town in the distance, he took a compass reading.

When they returned with the good news, a quick conference was held to decide what to do next. Jimmy gathered some blankets, cooking utensils, bread, butter, sausages and tea, that were quickly packed for Sergeant Miles to drop to John before night. An attached note advised that a rescue party would be with him around midday. Jimmy assumed that John was holding the fuel can up to indicate he had an engine fuel problem.

The rescue party consisted of Jimmy and the sergeant together with Mr Coles' best stockmen. They left at first light, carrying two cans of fuel and enough food and water for a day plus a land compass. The country alternated from treed hills to flat grasslands with cattle grazing. The stockmen skilfully led the party with only an occasional check of their direction with the compass.

They had to deviate several times over the hills but still made good time, enjoying a tea break after two hours' riding. They rode onto the river flat to find John half asleep under a wing. A few hearty handshakes and they decided to have a meal before examining the aircraft.

John was certain it was a fuel problem as the engine had backfired several times before stopping after he had selected the reserve fuel tank. The first thing they did was to drain the fuel tank through a chamois cloth.

It was an experimental fuel tank with a main compartment and a reserve compartment. The main compartment fuel was clear of water, but the reserve compartment had over a cup of water.

John's opinion was correct. After visually inspecting the inside of each fuel compartment to see if they were clean, they added fuel to each compartment. The fuel lines to the engine were drained. The engine was started and allowed to run for ten minutes.

Jimmy and Sergeant Miles both inspected the aircraft for damage and were satisfied it was fit for flight. The next problem was to fly the aircraft from the river flat. Jimmy and John paced the distance available for a safe take-off. It was marginal but the wind had increased over their selected take-off direction.

Together they pushed the aircraft back to the edge of the river flat and turned the aircraft to head into the wind. The men held the aircraft until the engine was at take-off power. When signalled by John, they let go.

With the engine roaring, the aircraft sped down the river flat until, at the very last moment, John pulled back on the control column and it gently climbed, heading for Mr Coles' farm. Those on the ground all cheered his take-off. The horse ride back was uneventful, and they arrived back at the farm at just after sundown.

The burning question was, "How did water get into the reserve fuel compartment?"

The mechanics and the pilots sat around the work bench. Jimmy started asking questions. 'I have several questions. First, who fuelled the aircraft and does anyone have any idea how water got into the reserve tank?'

One mechanic put up his hand. 'I filled the main fuel compartment. I definitely used a chamois to filter the fuel. There was no water.'

'Okay. Where did you get the fuel from?'

'I used the drum we always use. I have no idea how water got into the reserve tank compartment.'

A second mechanic then volunteered that he had topped up the reserve fuel compartment and said, 'I definitely used a chamois.'

Jimmy asked, 'Where did you get your chamois?'

He answered, 'It was on top of the fuel drum.'

'Where is it now?'

'Still there, I suppose. That's where I left it.'

The mechanic led Jimmy to the fuel drum and, yes, the chamois was still there. But it didn't look right. The material looked porous and too thin. Jimmy asked the sergeant to check the chamois.

The sergeant came back after a little while. 'I don't know what it is, but it won't filter water.'

The mechanic was shocked and sad. 'I'm sorry, sir. I didn't know.'

Jimmy said to him, 'Don't worry. At least we have found our problem. We now need to know where this material came from.'

John interrupted, 'Perhaps the pilots need to be more involved. This could be part my fault.'

Jimmy nodded, 'Yes, I agree. Pilots should be more involved.' After many questions, the source of the false chamois was not located and remained a mystery. The bulk fuel tank he had used was drained and found to have water in it. The fuel was syphoned to a clean tank through a chamois and would be used in future.

The following day the team was disbanded temporarily. Jimmy drove Sergeant Miles back to the railway station. He was happy; he had received a healthy cheque from Mr Coles.

Jimmy said,' Perhaps you might consider working here when we get up and running.'

He nodded. 'Yes, please keep me in mind. I've enjoyed working with you. Thank you and goodbye for now.'

Jimmy was now ready to put his dream into reality. He had kept abreast of the planned British Air Navigation Act and Regulations for Civil Flying and for the registration of aircraft and licencing of personnel. It was finally enacted on April 30th, 1921. The Australian Government soon followed the British Aviation Authority with the Air Navigation Act in 1921.

Jimmy had finalised his business plans and operational data, such as flight and maintenance manuals, technical records, staff structure and levels. He nominated himself as chief pilot and Ian Miles as chief engineer. He was ready to apply to operate an approved maintenance organisation and a flying training school in Mylonga.

The answer was disappointing. After waiting a month, he received a two-part answer. The government advised that they were not considering applications at this time for maintenance organisations or civil flying schools.

However, they were impressed with his submission and his British qualifications. They advised they would consider issuing him Australian licences in the near future as a maintenance engineer and a private pilot's licence based on his British licences and his experience with the military, the Avro Company and the Avro 504K aircraft over so many years.

Meanwhile, Mr Coles had approached the Australian Government to approve his paddock as a suitable airfield. Their answer to this was also disappointing. They advised they were only considering approving airfields to be used by airline operators with commercial contracts.

Where could he go from here? He had two serviceable British registered aircraft and a potential maintenance crew, but no airfield approval and no maintenance or operational approvals.

Mr Coles and Jimmy agreed to wait six months, then have a rethink of their plans, if the Australian Government would not grant their requested approvals.

A surprising alternative answer came in a lengthy three part telegram from Mr Sparks of the Avro Company. The Avro Company had been approached by the Australian Embassy in London, seeking their interest in establishing a company branch at the new Essendon Airport in Melbourne.

They advised, one or two operators were currently moving into Essendon Airport and if Avro were interested, they would hold an area of land for a hangar to be built for a maintenance organisation to be established.

Secondly, Mr Sparks advised that the company had received several orders for new aircraft from Australian customers. They were being crated ready for shipment the next week and could arrive within eight weeks, subject to Jimmy's availability.

Thirdly, Mr Sparks had received requests for contacts to carry out maintenance on Avro aircraft in Australia.

Your name came up in the discussion regarding aircraft maintenance. The Embassy staff knew of your applications to Melbourne. They advised they would accept your involvement in a new venture with Avro. You are obviously known in Australian aviation circles.

If you are interested in becoming a member of our new company work force, we would offer you the position of Manager – Arco Australia – a new company of ours. I realise setting up a new venture like this will be challenging, but I have confidence that you are up to the task. Please advise your thoughts and comments within seven days.

Signed, C. Sparks.

Jimmy sat with Jane on the porch, drinking beer and enjoying an evening snack. The night was balmy with clear skies. She had read the telegram but had not yet commented.

He said, 'I'll need the wisdom of Solomon to decide how to handle these two options.'

'Why? I see an easy answer. Tell Avro you will take the Arco position on condition you can take the two 504Ks with you.

'The business plans you have for here would be similar to the ones needed for Arco at Essendon. A few amendments here and there, I'm sure will suffice.'

He nodded. 'I'll ride over to Mr Coles tomorrow and tell him what's happened. I'll make my decision based on what he says.'

Mr Coles read the telegram. 'That's a lifetime appointment. I suggest you accept. We have no idea when, or if, we will ever be allowed to operate from here. Take the two aircraft to Essendon. At least they will be flown. I don't want them sitting and decaying here. I'll sign one over to your name and keep the other in the family in my name. You can operate and manage mine and donate my profits to the Royal Melbourne Hospital. I don't need the money.'

Jimmy sat there allowing Mr Coles' words to sink in. He responded, 'Thank you very much for the aircraft and your advice. I think you're correct. I'll contact Arco and tell them of our aircraft situation and let you know.'

He stuttered, 'I really–really don't know how to thank you for the aircraft.'

Mr Coles smiled. 'I'm happy to see the delight in your expression. That pleases me.'

Jimmy left and hurried to tell Jane of Mr Coles' comments and his *own* aircraft.

Jane said, 'I told you so; the problem is solved. Now you can concentrate on the Arco offer only.'

He sat down and thought of the words he would use in the telegram.

Mr C. Sparks.
Avro - Works Manager

Thank you for your telegram.

Item 1 – Yes, I am interested in your offer. If the hangar can be erected immediately – in time for the arrival of the crates, and the Arco Company (Aust.) is issued with an approval to carry out aircraft maintenance and I'm granted an Australian Aircraft Maintenance Engineers Licence with same endorsements as on my British Licence.

Items 2/3 – Yes, I can be available. I have a maintenance crew on standby, capable of assembling an aircraft and maintaining it.

N.B.   a. I would require financial assistance to relocate my family to Melbourne.

b. As you are no doubt aware, I have been involved with two 504k dual cockpit aircraft. I recently became an owner of one. I would like to bring these to Essendon, with your approval. I would suggest that these aircraft could be used as Arco demonstrators and possible pilot training.

I look forward to your response.

Jimmy Symons.

Jane read his response and agreed it was to the point, with no superfluous words.

Jimmy rode to town at first light the following morning to transmit the telegram.

The following week was taken up with preparation for the forthcoming shearing season. The shearing team's quarters had been cleaned thoroughly. The floor hosed and the oiled, the curtains washed and folded bedding placed on each bed. The dining area tables were cleaned, and the cooking area dusted and washed. The cooking and eating utensils had been washed and stowed after the last shearers had left. They were unwrapped and placed in the kitchen drawers.

At the end of the week, the eagerly awaited Avro telegram arrived.

Hello Jimmy,

Re-your telegram response.

1. *We have a contractor already building a hangar. It should be completed within a month and will be capable of holding six aircraft.*
2. *Yes, we agree to your requests. We would like you to start when the hangar is completed.*
3. *We will forward a contract for you to peruse. We have included your salary and a removal allowance.*
4. *Yes, bring your aircraft. It will save us the cost of shipping a low use demonstrator. We will pay a per flight fee for the aircraft and pilot, whom, I suggest, you organise on our behalf.*

Let me know your decision after you read the contract.

Signed, C. Sparks.

The contract was straight-forward and easy for a lay person to understand. Although he did show the contract to Mr Coles' solicitor and received a positive comment. He telegrammed Mr Sparks of his acceptance.

Jane was delighted with the telegram. Her only concern was where to live in Melbourne.

She had the address of several of her school friends and had advised them of her moving to Melbourne, asking their opinion of preferred areas near Essendon Airport. One former school friend, Kath Probert, wrote and advised, she and her husband owned a large guesthouse in Essendon and offered her family accommodation with them while she looked around for a house.

Jane decided to visit Kath and told her of her planned trip. She boarded a train to Melbourne, then transferred to another train to Essendon railway station. Even after six or seven years since they last met, they immediately recognised each other. They went to a nearby restaurant and chattered about their schooldays and their families.

Kath offered to take Jane to have a look at their guesthouse. As she drove her gig along the road from the station, Jane was surprised at the large houses in the suburbs. Not all were large, but a good number looked very expensive.

Kath lived in Essendon, not far from the new airport. The guesthouse was two-storied with two cottages at the rear. Jane was impressed with the cottages and preferred one of these rather the guest house.

Kath nodded. 'Yes, you can have either, long term if you wish.'

Jane said, 'Yes, let's agree now.' They shook hands. The cottage had two bedrooms and a veranda converted to a sleep-out. The lounge-dining room was big and there was a small kitchen. Jane felt Jimmy would agree with their new home.

The road was alongside a park and a lake with black swans. Adjacent the park was a primary school. Also, surprisingly, the road went straight to the airport. The location was ideal. Jane stayed overnight with Kath, who drove her to catch the next morning train home.

The family moved to Melbourne within the month. Jane was busy settling into the cottage. They looked forward to having many happy and rewarding years in Melbourne, with holidays back home in Mylonga every few months.

When Jimmy arrived in Melbourne, he visited solicitors, government offices and the airport. The business was progressing on time. He wanted all arrangements to be in order when the aircraft arrived.

When the crates arrived, Ian Miles had his team organised. He hired two of the men from Point Cook and two local trades assistants. Arco (Australia) was ready to go.

Jimmy's brother, John, had obtained a position in the local bank. It was a typical country bank. Two floors – the manager lived upstairs; the ground floor was the bank. Staffed by a manager, a senior teller and two other tellers. The manager had a secretary who occasionally assisted at the counter. Every customer was known personally to at least one of the bank staff. John enjoyed working there. They were all friendly and helpful when he first started, and he had recently been sent to Melbourne for a week's training at their head office.

He often accompanied the manager to the safe when large cash deposits or valuables were to be placed inside. Normally the manager kept the safe keys on his waistcoat watch chain. He only removed them when the safe needed to be opened.

Late Friday afternoon, a jeweller asked if the bank could mind five small gold ingots for the weekend, as his safe was rather small. John carried the five ingots to the safe while the manager opened it. After stowing the ingots, the manager placed his keys on his desk.

Just then a commotion was heard in the bank. Both the manager and John ran to the counter room to see two men fighting. One accused the other of jumping the queue. It took a few minutes to settle them down. They had both been drinking. The bank then returned to its normal quiet state.

The following Monday when the jeweller came to collect his ingots, the manager was shocked to find they were no longer in the safe. He immediately went to the police station only three buildings from the bank and reported it. How could this have happened? The keys had been with the manager all the time. Each of the staff were questioned, except the senior teller, who was off work with a broken arm.

The police were baffled. When re-reading statements from the staff, they noticed John's comment about the 'Keys being on the table'. The manager and John were re-interviewed, but it still didn't make sense.

The police sergeant said, 'There were only four of you here – the manager and John were together, and the clerk and the secretary were both at the front counter and the senior was away with a broken arm.'

The manager replied, 'No, he broke his arm that weekend, but he's trustworthy. He's had thirty exemplary years of service.'

The sergeant angrily replied, 'Why didn't you say so before? Incidentally have you ever had any thefts?'

The manager replied, 'Not that I know of.'

The secretary interrupted. 'Two years ago, two small bags of sovereigns were sent from here to Melbourne but didn't arrive.'

'Who was working here when it happened?'

'Only myself and the senior clerk,' she replied.

The police went to interview the senior clerk who denied any knowledge of theft of the ingots. He said he was in his office at the time of the fight.

In the meantime, the manager had called on the bank's locksmith to change the locks.

Next day he arrived and completed the lock replacement within an hour. As he was leaving he saw a small outdated safe in the corner. 'Do you still use it?'

He replied, 'No. I've been told the keys were lost several years ago and it's too small for our current requirements.'

'I'll soon find you a key. Give me an hour or so while I search for the model's key types.'

True to his word, the locksmith walked into the manager's office holding a key an hour later. 'Do want the honour of opening it after all these years? Who knowns what might be in it?'

The manager opened the safe and stood back in amazement. There were the missing ingots. He immediately locked the safe and sent John to fetch the police. When he reopened the safe, he stood back to let the police see the contents. The ingots were not the only items in there. They also found two bags of sovereigns. The manager then removed them to the main safe and relocked the old safe.

The police were certain the senior clerk was involved but there were many unanswered questions until the manager commented. 'The senior clerk is retiring in three months.' The police now had a motive.

The police decided to wire an alarm through a bolt hole in the back of the small safe and set the alarm unit up on the manager's upstairs balcony. Opening the safe door would set the alarm ringing.

A week later the senior clerk walked into the bank carrying a shopping bag, wanting to withdraw some money. He chose his visit at lunchtime when the manager was upstairs. The two tellers were busy, and the secretary was busy typing. After receiving his money, the senior clerk went to his office.

He then slipped into the room where the safes were and opened the small safe. The alarm immediately began ringing. By the time the senior clerk realised what had happened, the police were outside the bank, waiting for him.

The senior clerk sat down on the bank steps with his head in his hands.

The bank manager asked, 'Why? You have your own home, money and a good pension coming. You're a bloody fool.'

When the manager left the keys on his desk, the senior clerk saw them there and he took the opportunity of the fight to open both safes and transfer the ingots. The police found an original key to the small safe in his pocket.

However, there was a small complication – neither the bullion nor the ingots had been removed from the bank, so technically the bank had not been robbed. The charge ended up being 'Intent to defraud'.

The senior clerk was fired and lost his bank pension. John wondered why he was so dumb. Was it just greed or the challenge to see if he could beat the system?

After the court case, John wrote the story and had the secretary type it into a short story without any true names of the country town or persons. He sent a copy to Jimmy and Michael.

Michael enjoyed it so much he sent it to his Tours Publishers, and it sold several thousand copies throughout England. John was delighted to receive a cheque for his literary efforts.

Jane and Jimmy had two children. First a son, David, and then a girl, Marie. They both attended the nearby primary school and soon became popular. David was a good athlete and Marie showed musical skills.

The Arco Aviation Company had become successful. Jimmy's business plan had set a limit on accepted work, and this gained the company a reputation of on time performance. He was kept busy himself with his flying demonstrations for potential buyers and student instructions.

The children were now twelve and eleven years old. Jimmy decided to take a trip to the UK. He was tired and over fifty years old; he needed a holiday. When told, the children clapped their hands in delight. Although they knew little of the UK, they were excited that they were going on a ship.

Jane was pleased at his decision. She knew he was mentally worn out. He made the bookings and then advised Mr Sparks, who was retiring soon, of his plans. Ian Miles would be acting manager in Jimmy's absence.

The great day arrived. The ship sailed on a cold and overcast day. The children sat by a porthole. To keep the children occupied, each day before dinner, Jimmy had them write a small essay on what they had seen on that day. The children grumbled but did it. By the time they returned home, David would have completed four essay books and Marie three books.

Jimmy had seen most of the sights before but enjoyed being their tour guide. Jane had a box Brownie camera and had become an avid photographer. They went via Colombo and did a three-day stopover. They hired a tour guide and did a visit of tea plantations and different buildings.

They next stopped in Cairo for a four-day visit to the pyramids and the Sphinx.

Another Australian Eagle

On the ship's way to the UK, it was diverted to Naples to transfer some crew. The crews were transferred by a motorboat.

Early in the morning, Jimmy awakened the family to come on deck and see Sicily's two volcanos, Mt Etna and Stromboli lighting up the sky with the glow of their erupting gases and lava. The ship then steamed nonstop to Portsmouth. Before they left Portsmouth they visited Admiral Nelson's famous ship, the HMS Victory.

They travelled by train to London. They found London very busy, with narrow streets and shops everywhere. They stayed seven days in London.

On the first day David got lost. They had only walked past a few shops and he vanished. They spent half an hour searching for him and then went to a nearby police station to report him missing. Lo and behold, there was David sitting on the station counter, drawing a kangaroo.

The police sergeant laughed. 'We get a lost child nearly every day.' It was laughter and not tears.

After seeing the Changing of the Guard at the Palace they visited the Victoria and Albert Museum.

They then travelled by train to Manchester to visit the Avro Company and Mr Sparks. Over the past years they had communicated frequently and often written about their family as well.

Jimmy drove up to the airfield entry where a young guard enquired about his business. When he mentioned his name, the guard said, 'My father knew you when you first came here. He often mentioned the young Australian technical officer. My father's name was Mr James. He was the administration manager. He passed away last year.'

Jimmy nodded. 'Yes, I remember your father. He was a great help to me when I first arrived. He made my introduction to the company very easy. I guess many things have changed since those days.'

The guard nodded and said, 'Here's your pass for you and your family. Follow the yellow line. Have a good day, sir.'

There were a few changes, but generally the buildings were the same as he had drafted twenty years ago on the master plan.

Mr Sparks was expecting Jimmy and his family. They shook hands and he introduced Jane and the children.

Mr Sparks had rearranged the boardroom into a dining room. His wife was there and Shirley Blake who had been his secretary for many years.

The luncheon was excellent, and the conversation was the same as any family gathering. Even the children joined in. When dessert was served, Mr Sparks or now, Charles, and Jimmy left the room for a quick chat regarding business.

Charles asked, 'We're unsure of our future. There is considerable competition. These new companies will one day have an effect. It will happen, but I think we can continue for a few more years as we are.'

Jimmy nodded. 'Large commercial aircraft are coming and will be more sophisticated and they will be government supported.'

Charles stood up. 'Yes, changes are coming. Which way we go will be up to the board. I think Arco Aviation will continue as per your current operation. Now, we should join the others.'

After bidding farewell and promising to keep in touch, the Symons family drove north to Carlisle, where Jimmy's mother's parents had been born. After asking for directions at the local village hall, they located the original farmhouse. Her forefathers were yeomen farmers. They had been granted the land by King Henry the Eighth in 1546.

Jane nearly ran out of film. She had taken over a hundred photographs so far.

It was now time to return home. They had been away from home for nearly three months. They travelled to Liverpool and within three days they were sailing en route to Melbourne via Cape Town. The weather south to Cape Town was miserable – overcast, cold and drizzling rain. Most days they stayed in their cabin and read, played cards or slept. The children were updating their logbooks. They even had their meals in their cabin.

A day out from Cape Town the skies cleared, and the temperature increased. The family was standing on the deck watching Table Mountain appear in the distance. It was an imposing sight. A large flat rock nearly four thousand feet above sea level, overlooking Cape Town.

The ship's captain advised the passengers the ship would depart in two days after loading water, fresh food and dropping off and picking up mail.

Jimmy and the family went ashore in the ship's workboat with six other passengers. They hired a car for half a day to see the local sights.

That afternoon, they went for a stroll along the waterfront shops. Most were souvenir shops and sold local native artifacts and other African local items of interest.

Jane opened her handbag to purchase a print, when a young native grabbed her bag and ran.

He only travelled twenty yards when a large African policeman swung his arm out straight, hitting the robber in the throat. The robber fell backwards and laid flat on his back on the ground, semi-conscious.

Jimmy had started to chase the robber and was amazed at the action of the policeman. It was so professional. The policeman picked up Jane's handbag and handed it to her. 'All in a day's work, madam.'

He raised his helmet and walked away, vanishing into the gathering crowd, leaving the robber groaning on the ground.

Jimmy had not had a chance to thank the policeman. After the drama, they were very popular at dinner that evening. The ship sailed the next morning non-stop to Melbourne and home!

The family was eagerly looking forward to the end of their travelling. It had been an enjoyable adventure of a lifetime but after four months, home was where they wanted to be now.

After a few days stay at Mylonga, meeting the families again, they returned to Essendon and school and work.

The two children were good students and David won the local district three mile running race and had his photo in the Age newspaper.

During Jimmy's absence, Ian Miles had carried out his acting manager role exceptionally well and was given a generous bonus. The company was in good shape and respected in the Australian aviation industry.

Jimmy had now accumulated over four thousand flying hours.

As the years rolled along, he had been required to be tested to fly newer aircraft, to keep abreast with the current models. The days of fabric fuselages and wooden propellors were nearly over. Aluminium aircraft were now being introduced with metal propellors, improved instrument panels and navigation systems were being developed. He was grateful he had been involved in the fledgling industry those many years ago and had seen the industry continue to develop. His theory on the wedge-tailed eagle's wings were now being explored. Where would it end?

He was now a wealthy man. He had achieved his boyhood dream of an aviation career, had a loving wife and two happy and healthy children. What more could a man ask for?

The team had a busy week – five one-hundred hourly checks, two engine changes and one demonstration flight, plus some minor maintenance.

The mechanics had closed the hangar doors and gone home. Jimmy, as usual, did his secondary security check of the aircraft.

Tomorrow was ANZAC Day and a public holiday which was a welcome break from work. He sat in his office and looked at a photograph dated November 1919. It was the only photograph of Ida, Terry and himself in military uniform – Ida, in her nurse's uniform of grey skirt, jacket, matching bonnet and a red cape with her three medals and oakleaf, Terry in his Light Horse uniform and three medals, and finally Jimmy in Light Horse uniform with pilot wings and military cross and three war medals.

That year was when Mylonga held its first ANZAC Day march and Commemorative Service. A small committee sat down and planned the dual event. There were thirty-five locals who had served overseas in WW1 and five from the Boer War. All agreed to attend.

The district had a pipe band comprised of locals from three nearby towns. The committee advertised the march route, ending at the local sports oval. Volunteers were plentiful – road marshallers, food stall attendants and, most importantly, an M.C., a minister and readers for the service. All was in order for the memorable day.

The day arrived with clear skies and only a light breeze. At ten o'clock the stirring sounds of the bagpipes and drums were heard. The spectators started cheering and clapping. The band marched into the main street, followed by three soldiers in uniform. The middle soldier carried the Australian flag, and the others carried a rifle with a fixed bayonet. They were followed by two identical cars carrying the Boer War veterans. Next came a lieutenant leading the marching veterans three abreast. A single car was next with the two local nurses – Ida and school friend. The biggest round of applause was for the six Light Horsemen lead by Jimmy, then four horsemen in line, with Terry bringing up the rear. Then came the local Light Horse Militia with their flag pennant, parading in threes and looking very professional. The spectators were delighted and proud of the marchers, shouting their praise.

When the parade reached the sports oval, they were dismissed. The participants then joined their families and friends for the service. It was a low key and subdued service. The speeches were carefully worded. There were too many bad memories. Most just listened with their own private thoughts.

The three friends met many times after the war. They spoke of their bad days and good days. It helped the three of them cope with their demons. None of them discussed the traumas they had seen or endured with their families or friends. The three friends had a bond like no other.

Jimmy sat smiling to himself, recalling those memorable days of long ago – his trip to England as a young man, being hired by Avro, learning to be a technical officer and a pilot, his flights to France, his dramatic flights in the desert and then joining the Light Horse. Should he write his story? A distant car horn interrupted his memories.

He sighed, stood up, left his office and switched off

the building's lights. He locked the main entry door and walked to his parked car, nodding 'Good night' to the security guard.

The company had purchased a car for his personal use eight years ago. It was an A Model Ford sedan. He enjoyed the car even if it did have a few blind spots. He needed to be alert when joining into traffic on narrow or single lane roads. He was still thinking how lucky life had been for both he and Jane.

As he pushed the choke cable in, he had a quick look to his right and turned into the exit road. He did not see the truck approaching. It hit his car on the driver's side, killing him instantly.

CAPTAIN JAMES THOMAS
1884 – 1936
Ex – Australian Light Horse.
'The Eagle has flown.'

EPILOGUE

In 1942 at Point Cook, a cadet pilot passing out parade was being conducted. An air vice marshal was reading through the names and noted a name that drew his attention – David Symons. He wondered. He asked his aide to find out where David Symons was standing in the lined-up assembly.

As the air vice marshal walked past the assembled cadets, he stopped several times and said a few words of encouragement to them. When he reached David, he asked, 'Would you be related to a Jimmy Symons?'

'Yes', answered David. 'He was my father.'

The air vice marshal nodded. 'I flew with your father. He was a great man. He would be pleased that you are following in his footsteps. I'm sure we will meet again.'

David felt most proud. They did meet again.

Two years later David was flying a Douglas C47 freighter from Cairns to Port Moresby. On arrival he was told he would have three VIPs to transport to Goroka in the New Guinea highlands. When he was introduced to them, he immediately recognised the air vice marshal from his cadet days at Point Cook.

The AVM smiled and said, 'I told you we would meet again,' and shook his hand.

That night in the mess, he sat with David for several hours and recalled his heady days in WW1 with his father.

David was only twelve years of age when his father had died, and he knew little of his WW1 days. The next morning, they flew back to Cairns. David would never forget that evening with the AVM. Hearing of his father's exploits from a man he served with was uplifting. He felt so proud.

After Jimmy's tragic death, Jane and the children moved back to the farm. She leased the two aircraft to Arco (Aust). The company presented her with a handsome cheque in appreciation of Jimmy's service to the Avro Company (albeit Arco). She did not remarry and stayed on the farm with her two children, together with her memories.

David and Marie both went to local schools and received good grades.

David joined the RAAF as soon as he was old enough. Marie was destined to become a local farmer's wife. Uncle Michael did not return to Mylonga. His ship was torpedoed towards the end of the war, and he was declared lost at sea.

The family was only advised in November 1920 – two years after the sinking of his ship. As Michael had not married, he bequeathed his estate to Thomas, his brother, and the local hospital.

The Symons family name lives on in Mylonga due to Michael Symons. The money he bequeathed to the local hospital went towards the establishment of an emergency ward, on one condition – that it was named, 'The Symons Memorial Ward'.

NOTES

Note 1   Wing tip feathers

The latest design modern jet aircraft have the tips of their wings turned upwards, almost vertical, such as the Boeing 747-400 and the Airbus A340. This reduces wing tip drag, by smoothly merging the upper wing faster airflow with the lower wing slower moving airflow at the wing tip. The two airflows at the wing tips of aircraft with flat wing tips, such as the B707, creates air turbulence drag and subsequent reduced flight efficiency.

Note 2   Suez Canal

In the second century AD, a canal was constructed from the River Nile to the Red Sea. By the seventh century it had silted up. It was reopened in 641 until 767 when war closed it. It had been called the River of Trajan. The town of Ismailia was built during the construction of the Suez Canal by Ferdinand De Lesseps in 1865 which opened as a single canal. There are now duplicated canals from the Red Sea to Cairo.

Note 3   Avro 504K Specifications

Designed by – Allice Vernon Roe
Manufactured in Manchester and several overseas countries.
Capacity – two crew – no armament or pilot and Lewis gun.
Twin wing – Trainer dual seater. Later, single seat.
Wooden 2-blade propellor – 9 ft dia. and pitch 8 ft 8 ins.

Engine

Universal engine – mount fitted.
100 hp Gnome Monosoupape/110 hp Le Rhone.
Wings with struts.
Span 36 feet
Height 10.5 feet
Wing area 330 feet
Length 27.5 feet
Fuel tank – 25 imperial gallons
Ceiling – 18000 feet
R.O.C. 700 feet per min. 10,000 feet in 16 mins.

Weights

Max. 1800 lbs/1824 lbs
Empty 1230 lbs

Speed – 83 mph at 6500 feet/93 mph

Endurance – 3 hours – 250 miles

Body – Square fuselage. Wooden frames and canvas covered – sewn and then painted to shrink onto frame (less drag).
Two wheels and centre skid. Tail skid.

Note 4   Hansom Cabs

Hansom cabs were often called our 'first taxies'. They were a two wheeled, covered, single-horse coach. The coachman sat outside and at the rear. His seat was high, enabling him to see the road ahead.

Note 5   Touch and Goes

This aviation term is mainly used when a trainee pilot is practising his take-off and landing skills in an aircraft. His instructor will require a trainee pilot after he has taken off from an airfield, to fly around and land his aircraft and without stopping, immediately take off again. That is, he has to *touch* the landing field and *go* round again.

AUTHOR

John P. F. Lynch was educated at St. Bernard's CBC College, Moonee Ponds Victoria.

He is the great, great grandson of Kyneton pioneer Joseph Hall who established Windmill Farm in 1849. He built two other nearby local farms in the 1850's.

He has written several history/fictional and local Victorian history books, plus his autobiography. Most books are available in local state libraries and as e-books. Primarily the stories are based on Victorian colonial and WW1 events with possible interrelated scenarios. To research these books, he successfully travelled to his family's origins in England and Ireland several times.

John is an ex-navy veteran and was President of the Romsey/Lancefield R.S.L. for nearly ten years. He is a Reserve member of the Macedon Ranges Legacy Group, having served as Chairman of the group, long term Sergeant of Arms and a Board Member of the Bendigo Club.

He served on the Romsey Football/Netball Club committee for over twelve years as President/Secretary and committee member.

Currently he is the Technical Advisor to the Craigieburn War Memorial Remembrance Committee, having previously served as Vice President. He is a Life Member of several of these associations.

He is a Member of the Order of Australia, a Knight of the Order of St John of Jerusalem and a Fellow of the Royal Victorian Association of Honorary Justices.

He is now retired and lives with his wife in the Highlands Retirement Village in Craigieburn, Victoria,

OTHER BOOKS

By John P. F. Lynch

The Convict and the Soldier
The Aborigine and the Drover
The Constable and the Miner
The Shearer and the Magistrate
Twice Wounded

VICTORIAN LOCAL HISTORY

St Mary's Parish – 1858 to 2006
The Romsey/Lancefield R.S.L. – 1933 to 2008
The Romsey Football/Netball Club – 1878 to 2009
Joseph Hall – Kyneton – 1804 to 1872

AUTOBIOGRAPHY

A Lifetime's Journey